HERALD OF THE WORD

ARNOLD JANSSEN

HERALD OF THE WORD

E. J. EDWARDS, S.V.D.

MISSION PRESS, S.V.D.
TECHNY, ILLINOIS

Imprimi potest
  A. GR. KAPPENBERG, S.V. D.
    Superior General
  January 6, 1951

Imprimatur
  ✠ SAMUEL CARDINAL STRITCH
    Archbishop of Chicago
  March 1, 1951

PRINTED IN THE
UNITED STATES OF AMERICA

TO

THE

MEN AND WOMEN

WHO FOLLOW

ARNOLD JANSSEN

IN THE

LOVE OF THE HOLY SPIRIT

AND

IN THE

SERVICE OF THE DIVINE WORD

TO

THE

MEN AND WOMEN

WHO FOLLOW

ARNOLD JANSSEN

IN THE

LOVE OF THE HOLY SPIRIT

AND

IN THE

SERVICE OF THE DIVINE WORD

The factual material for this book

has been derived from

THE LIFE OF ARNOLD JANSSEN

by H. Fischer, S.V.D.

translated by F. M. Lynk, S.V.D.

and

THE SPIRITUALITY OF OUR FOUNDER

by H. Sandkamp, S.V.D.

Grateful acknowledgment is hereby

made to the authors of these

original works

In obedience to the decree
of Pope Urban VIII and other sovereign Pontiffs, the
writer declares that the graces and other supernatural
facts related in this volume as witnessing to the sanctity
of Servants of God other than those canonized or be-
atified by the Church, rest on human authority alone;
and in regard thereto, as in all things else, the writer
submits himself without reserve to the infallible judgment of the Apostolic See, which alone has power and
authority to pronounce as to whom rightly belong the
Character and Title of Saint or Blessed.

Chapter 1

IT WAS late evening in the little Dutch border town of Nymwegen. At the customs' gate a pair of officials were finishing their inspection of a heavily laden wagon's contents. Nearby stood the owner of the wagon, a sturdy, broad-shouldered, plain looking sort of man, his eyes patiently, quietly watching them.

The officials scrambled down from the wagon their inspection completed. One of them spread some documents flat against the side of the wagon and stamped them energetically with a small rubber stamp. He went over to the driver and handed him the documents. "Everything is in order, sir," he announced.

Respectfully the driver thanked him, took the documents and carefully placed them in the inside pocket of his jacket. With deliberate step he went over to his wagon and clambered aloft to the driver's seat. He picked up the reins, turned to the officials and gave them a formal little nod of farewell, then slapped the

1

reins along the backs of his team. Slowly the wagon moved across the border into Germany.

For a moment the place was empty of traffic. One of the customs officers, a young man just come to this post, gazed idly at the solitary vehicle plodding along the flat dusty road. "Where is that fellow from?" he asked his older companion.

"Goch ... a little place ... about twenty miles from here."

"That's a valuable cargo he's hauling in that wagon."

"He's a reliable man. You'll get to know him. You get to know all of them after awhile — the ones you've got to watch, the ones you can trust. This one's all right."

"What's his name?"

"Gerard Janssen. He's got a small farm and a big family."

"A farmer? What's he doing in this hauling business then?"

"Needs the cash. I told you he had a big family."

"I'd want money pretty bad before I'd risk my neck hauling a cargo like that at night — alone."

His companion gave him a curious look. "He doesn't travel alone."

The young official lifted a questioning glance. It had been very evident that Janssen was the only one on the wagon. "You mean he goes armed?"

"Well, I guess you could call it that. But he doesn't carry any gun or knives or that sort of thing." A puzzled frown creased the young man's brow, but the older official did not see it. He was gazing off in the distance at the wagon. "Look," he ordered.

2

The young man turned his gaze down the road. The wagon had come to a halt. The man was clambering down from the driver's seat. For a moment he stood in the roadway, fumbling something out of his pocket; then he took hold of the reins with one hand, and the conveyance started up again, the driver pacing along beside the horses.

The young man turned to the older official. "What was that for?"

"He always does that after he gets out a ways."

"What is he doing?"

"Praying."

"Praying?" The young man's face could not have shown more shocked amazement if his companion had calmly told him that a contraband article had gotten past his inspection. He was not exactly irreligious, but, according to his view of the matter, praying was something a man did in church, or when he was dying, not while he was at work.

The older official was smiling at his evident amazement, and he turned away from that, and gazed back again at this strange teamster who prayed while he worked. Dusk was settling over the flat countryside, and through the wan light and lengthening shadows walked the figure of that man, by the side of his wagon, a dim solitary figure far off in the dwindling distance.

* * *

The stillness of evening lay over the land as Gerard Janssen plodded by the side of his team. There was only the creak of the wagon beneath its load, and the crunch of the wheels against the hard surface of the highway.

The dark came on quickly. He stopped and lighted a lantern and hung it at the side of his wagon. Patiently he plodded along, praying aloud, the beads of his rosary slipping through the work-hardened fingers. The dark of the night was all about him, and through it there went the one small light from his wagon-lantern, bobbing steadily beside him. "And the light shines in darkness; and the darkness grasped it not." Always that thought came to him when walking like this at night. And in his soul of simple faith he felt the poignancy of grief and sorrow that must have torn the great Heart of the Christ who came to bring light to a world of utter darkness. But the people of the darkness had loved the darkness more than they loved the light. It must have been pitifully lonely to be a light shining in darkness. The darkness made a hard wall about the light. He looked at his little lantern, and thought that here, too, was a little light shining in a great darkness. And he felt strangely content and satisfied to be like the One who had come unto His own and His own had not known him. For the Light did not die. Here and there in the great blackness other small lights were kindled, and in time all the world would blaze with the glory of it.

His beads were finished, and there was no longer the sound of his voice tolling his prayer, but only the creak of the wagon and the crunch of its wheels on the road. He halted the conveyance and tiredly mounted to the seat. The thought of home and food and rest was good. Through the dark of the night the lights of Goch glimmered before him, small warm little squares of radiance. He loved his native village with that deep tenacious

4

affection of a son of the soil. Here he had been born and reared and his fathers before him.

He had no wealth, no learning. He could read and write and keep his modest accounts. That had been all his schooling. His life had been mostly work, hard work, unending work, work for small profit. But he had been blessed with a wife who was a saint. An affectionate smile crossed his wearied countenance as he thought of Anna. She seemed always praying, and yet she did the work of a dozen. He had his home and his children, a goodly number of children. He would not be able to give them any of the finer things of life — higher education, a distinguished name or a financial start in the business world. But that did not disturb him although he loved each of them dearly. Children were like seeds. Each of them destined for an individual growth. He would give them what he had; the expansion and growth must be their own. A love of work, a love for God — these were the things by which he had lived. He gave them that by example, by word of mouth, by training. What they did with them in later life would be their concern, but he had the farmer's trust in the goodness of the seed. From the firm seed of healthy wheat there did not bloom thistles and thorns, and from industrious, religious children there could only come real men and women.

He took out a watch and held it beneath the lantern. He was coming close to the edge of the village and he was on time. Some of the children would be waiting him. As though in answer to his thought, two boys came running toward him from the shadows of a clump of trees. He halted the wagon and they clambered up beside him. Arnold sat next to him, William at the edge of the seat.

"You are safely here, Father," exclaimed William, looking over his shoulder at the contents of the wagon. "Nothing was lost or — or stolen?"

"No, nothing was lost or stolen."

"We prayed with mother that no one would molest you," said Arnold.

"Thank you, son," he replied gravely. "No one molested me."

"Is there gold in all those boxes?" asked William, peering intently at the heaped up cargo in back of him.

"You are not to ask, William," reprimanded his father. "There are valuable things in the boxes. I told you that. Thank God that they have arrived safely." William murmured a subdued agreement, and for a while there was silence. Then Arnold spoke up in his quiet voice.

"I wish you would not have to carry such things, Father," he said. "It is better to be carrying only salt from Geldern and Staelen each week. It is not dangerous. No one would think of harming you if you carried only salt."

"There is no need to fear. I am always protected. You know that. When you pray there is nothing to fear."

Arnold was silent and the wagon creaked onward and rounded a corner. A glass-protected niche at the corner of a street held the picture of the Blessed Virgin. This was the Street of Our Lady (Frauenstrasse) and on this street was their home. It was an old teamster's house which successive generations of the Janssen family had occupied. Gerard Janssen had a small farm, but this house was his main source of livelihood. It functioned not only as the office for conducting his teamster

6

business but also served as a salt depot for the wholesale market. Over and above that it was his home. Above the door hung a sign with a curry comb indicating the teaming business.

He drew the wagon to a halt, and the boys and he dismounted and entered the house.

Chapter 2

TO THE casual visitor Goch is an insignificant town. It is not only small and dull but it leaves the impression that it will remain always small and boringly dull. Nothing could possibly ever happen in the confines of so staid a town. And yet its Stone-Gate, flanked by two round towers, could tell a different story. This town had once been a fortress. This little town had in the course of its existence seen a great deal of bustle, confusion and stirring events.

Originally the town had been the center of a considerable wool and linen industry, and its people were well-to-do. Then came the Thirty Years' War, and, up to the middle of the eighteenth century, the little town was in the midst of the maelstrom. Time and again, soldiers from the different warring states pillaged the whole region, pestilence swept over the town, poverty and famine stalked its streets, and the population gradually dwindled away. But the town would not die.

There was a tough, rugged strain in its farmer folk that held out against all adversity.

The Napoleonic Wars repeated the town's tribulations. Five times the little village changed masters. But it endured. And when the wars were ended and a period of peace ensued it emerged from its ruins, and, by slow steps, began to rebuild.

Gerard Janssen was a child of this period. His youth was bound up with hard work and poverty. His father had died when he was very young, and he had been cared for by his grandfather. At the age of seventeen he took charge of the small farm and the teamster business which his grandfather was no longer able to conduct. Despite his own inexperience and the impoverished condition of the country, he had managed to eke out a living for the family from the project. But the trials and toil of his youth made of him a serious-minded man.

The little town with its Stone-Gate, his small house and farm, the flat roads leading to the Dutch border towns, that was all the world he knew. In the course of time he met and married a girl from a neighboring village, Anna Catherine Wellesen. He brought his bride to Goch and then, under the same roof where his forefathers had dwelt, he raised his family and worked for their support.

The simple outlook he had on life, his uncomplaining acceptance of the unending work and toil was something that had been part of their family for generations. It was the way his family had lived, it was the way he lived. It was sufficient for him. But there was in this hard and fast adherence to the spirit of the past nothing of apathetic fatalism, but the vivid, deep conviction

9

that their attitude toward life and work was good and right, and worthy to be held at all costs.

As a child he had sat at the fireside of an evening and listened to the stories of the men and women who had suffered so heroically for their faith during the Religious Wars. There were familiar names among them, for Goch, despite its staid appearance, had contributed its share of courageous, quiet-eyed heroes. They were a glory to the town, and stories of their devotion lit the lamp of highest adventure in his young heart. And now, as a grown-up man, he would sit of an evening by the fireside and re-tell to his own children the stories that he had heard as a child, and watch the quiet glow come into the eyes about him.

This was their heritage — a history of storm and strife, a life of faith and prayer, of poverty and courage. His own youth had been bound up, and still was, with the aftermath of those days of struggle and heroism. They, too, were sharers in it, and he wanted none of them to be unmindful of what had gone on before. The hard, enduring earth had no personal pride in the qualities that enable it to survive drought and fire, cold and storm; and in his own soul there was no vain complacency for the constancy and firmness that had brought his family and him through the years of trial and want. There was only this dogged conviction about the supreme facts of faith and prayer. Storms meant nothing, for they could be put to use, to good use, as everything could, by prayer.

And when he had finished his recital, and when the children had talked among themselves and questioned him to their heart's content, he would signify that it was time to go to bed. Then all of them would be

10

marshalled in a row, even as he had been when a child, and would kneel before the family altar for night prayers. He himself knelt at the head of the line, his wife at his side. The children knelt in the order of seniority: Margaret, Arnold, Gerard, William, Peter, Gertrude, Theodore and John. He looked down the line of young heads.

"Whose turn is it?" he asked.

"Mine," replied Arnold.

"Begin then," ordered his father.

Arnold cleared his throat, made the sign of the cross, and began to recite the beads.

Just as they were finishing the third decade there came a loud knock upon the door. Arnold looked at his father. "Wait a minute," ordered his father. He stood up, went to the door, and opened it. One of their neighbors, Mr. Braun, stood there. Mr. Janssen pushed wide the door. "Come in, Mr. Braun."

"Thank you. I'm glad to see you got back safely." He twisted his hat nervously in his hands. "The — the shipment is in good order?"

There were some boxes of gold for the merchants of the town in the shipment, and a goodly portion of it belonged to Mr. Braun. He trusted Janssen. The man was honest. But the thought of all his gold lying unprotected overnight filled his soul with uneasy qualms. He wanted those boxes under his own lock and key before he went to bed.

"Everything is safe, Mr. Braun," assured his host quietly, "and you're just in time. We were saying the rosary and you can pray with us. It will do you good."

Before he knew what had happened, Mr. Braun found himself kneeling beside his big-bodied host.

There was a Litany of the Blessed Virgin being recited, the responses filling the plain room's quietness with their lulling smoothness. Automatically his voice joined in: "Pray for us ... Pray for us ... Pray for us." But his mind was still with the boxes.

Suddenly Mrs. Janssen's voice, a low gentle admonition, cut across the prayer's smooth monotone. "William!" William's sleep-drowsy head nodded on unheedingly. She reached over and gently shook him. "William," she admonished. His eyes flew open. "Go kneel by your father."

William stumbled to his feet and made his way shamefacedly to the side of his father. Very gingerly he knelt beside his parent, his eyes now wide open and alert.

The prayer had stopped. "Sleep during prayer," said his mother, "comes from the devil; he does not like prayer, and he tries his best to make us fall asleep." There was silence for a moment.

"Go ahead, Arnold," ordered his father. The prayers went on to their conclusion. Then all paused, and suddenly Gerard Janssen's voice spoke alone.

"In the beginning was the Word,
and the Word was with God;
and the Word was God.
He was in the beginning with God.
All things were made through him,
and without him was made
nothing that has been made.
In him was life,
and the life was the light of men.
And the light shines in the darkness;

12

and the darkness grasped it not.
There was a man,
one sent from God,
whose name was John.
This man came as a witness,
to bear witness concerning the light,
that all might believe through him.
He was not himself the light,
but was to bear witness to the light.
It was the true light
that enlightens every man
who comes into the world.
He was in the world,
and the world was made through him,
and the world knew him not.
He came unto his own,
and his own received him not.
But to as many as received him
he gave the power of becoming sons of God;
to those who believe in his name:
Who was born not of blood,
nor of the will of the flesh,
nor of the will of man,
but of God.
And the Word was made flesh,
and dwelt among us.
And we saw his glory —
glory as of the only-begotten of the Father —
full of grace and of truth."

For a moment there was silence, then all made the
sign of the cross and stood up. Painfully, Mr. Braun
got to his feet. The family were moving about, talking

13

quietly. Gerard Janssen laid hold of his arm with a friendly clasp. "You feel a lot better after a bit of prayer, don't you?"

Mr. Braun scratched his head. "A bit of prayer? Well, a bit of prayer is all right, neighbor, but there seems to be no end to your prayers. Did you have to recite the whole gospel with it, too?" Janssen looked at him. "I mean that last part. That was the Gospel of St. John, wasn't it?"

"Oh, yes. But it was just the opening part of the Gospel of St. John. It's a strong prayer, Mr. Braun," he confided, "and it has great power with God."

Mr. Braun stared a moment at the plain serious face of Gerard Janssen, and then, as though embarrassed by the seriousness of his host, turned his gaze away. One of the boys, Arnold, was standing by his father's side.

"I never thought of it as a prayer," said Mr. Braun. "It's kind of hard to understand. Except maybe one or two sentences."

"It's a prayer, the best. You ought to try it some time."

Mr. Braun mumbled something, and then directed the conversation quickly to his precious consignment of valuables. The two men moved over to the table and Mr. Janssen drew some papers out of his pocket.

Arnold stood there a moment, his mind busied with the words his father had spoken. Many times, he, too, had wondered about that long prayer that his father thought so much of. His father's second name was John, Gerard John. He had been born on the feast of St. John the Evangelist and he had a great devotion for his patron saint. Perhaps that was why he had taken the first part of St. John's Gospel and made of it a

14

prayer. It was not like most of the prayers which Arnold knew. It did not ask for anything. And yet in time of affliction, or sickness, or trouble on the farm, his parents would unfailingly have recourse to that prayer. One of his earliest memories was of a terrifying thunderstorm that whipped the flat countryside with wind and water and terrible bolts of lightning. In the midst of it the family were grouped about their father, all of them kneeling before the small crucifix and a lighted candle, while their father's voice calmly, confidingly recited the beginning of the Gospel of St. John. That experience had been repeated many times. His father had told him it was a prayer to keep all of them from harm and their crops from damage. And always they had emerged from the danger of the storm untouched, their fields drenched with the fecund rain that brought greater harvests.

The prayer had become part of his youth, identified with it as a powerful resource that could be called into use when everything else was of no avail. He had grown to love the sonorousness of its solemn phrases, the poignancy of its tragic rejection of the Light by human darkness, the mysteriousness of its language that probed back to the ultimate reality of God and the wonders of His design for man and their redemption.

15

Chapter 3

AS A BOY Arnold was light of build and rather delicate, but the frail body housed a very active mind. Although he was the smallest boy in his class his exceptional diligence soon placed him at the head of his fellow-students. As a result the quiet, unassuming youngster received more than one good thump in the ribs from envious classmates. This was to remind him that if he was a bit better than they mentally, they were still his superior muscularly.

There was a retired old priest in the town by the name of Father Lax, and when Arnold had learned how to be an altar boy he was delegated to be this priest's Mass server. Each morning Arnold would meet Father Lax at his house, carry the chalice for him to church, serve his Mass, and then accompany him home after Mass. The priest's housekeeper would fill his pockets with fruit to reward him "for serving Mass so devoutly."

Although so young and his health anything but robust, he had his share of little chores about the farm and home. One of his tasks was to drive the cows to pasture in the morning, and to herd them back into the barns in the evening.

At 5:00 o'clock each morning his mother would wake him, help him dress and say his morning prayers. After this he had a large glass of milk with bread and butter. The cows were all tied together and the little cowherd would trot along after them to the pasture.

Every one in the Janssen houschold had their work, and ample amounts of it. But it was his father's way to so tie in their work with their faith that it took away much of the drudgery from the toil. The boys would carry a copy of the catechism in a pocket when they went to work and in a leisure moment would memorize one of the questions and answers. Their father would not only work with them, pray with them and share moments of leisure with them, he would also quite frequently catechize them.

Late one Monday afternoon he came through the pasture in which Arnold was rounding up the cattle. He watched him a moment, noticing the catechism tucked in his back pocket. Then he called him.

Arnold came up to him. "Yes, Father?"

"You served Mass well, this morning, son," he said. "Father Lax is old and slow, but he is a good priest." His gaze fixed intently on the boy. "You know what this week is?"

"Ember week."

"What does that mean?"

"Wednesday, Friday and Saturday are days of fast and abstinence."

17

"And also of special prayer. Pray for good priests, son. There is no greater blessing for a parish than a good priest. A parish that has one is rich."

"Yes, Father," replied the boy. "I'll pray for good priests."

A smile came over his face at the earnestness of the boy's reply. "There is much of your mother in you," he said.

The boy said nothing for a moment, only his eyes showing the pleasure which his father's words had brought to him. He was always happy to have done something to make his father smile, and a word of praise from this strong, serious man was like an accolade. He drew closer to his father and took his hand. "Father," he said, "there is something I want to ask you."

"Ask away."

"I saw you at Mass this morning. You always go to Mass on Mondays, but not on the other weekdays. Why is that?"

"Well, son, there is no time really for me to go to Mass on any of the weekdays."

"I know that," replied the boy, "but you go on Mondays."

"Yes. I do. In honor of the Holy Spirit, son. Even if the work on the farm has to suffer I won't miss that Mass on Monday. It is too important." His face slowly lighted up. "You see, Arnold, it is the Holy Spirit who brings comfort and strength to a man's soul and peace to his family. You see the bright sunlight on the meadow here, the grain over there in the field starting to get heavy and ripe. He does that. Brightness, joy, increase — that's His doing. And He does the same for a man's soul. He can fill your heart with joy and make it strong and eager to do good deeds."

Arnold looked wonderingly up at him. The little burst of enthusiastic words was an unusual thing coming from this plain, stalwart father of his.

His father put a work-worn hand gently on the boy's shoulder. "You know now why I go to Mass on Mondays, son." The rough palm patted his shoulder. "Run along now, and get those cattle into the barn."

Arnold went back obediently to his work. He herded the cows into the barn and bedded them down for the night. Later, his father would bring in the team of horses and he would have to tend and feed them. The horses were owned by his father, but the major part of the farm that they tilled was rented. The family never could have subsisted on the meager income that their farm work brought in. That was why his father had to conduct a teaming business. It meant work, hard work, to make ends meet.

For years the boy was to be a witness and a sharer in the hard toil that was needed in order to wrest from the earth the bread of life. And across all those years there walked the figure of his father, stalwart, plainly dressed, a man who loved simplicity in all things. His honesty was a byword. There were opportunities aplenty for him to turn a quick dollar on his trips across the border into Holland. Petty smuggling is no recent invention, and then, as now, it could be quite lucrative. He made it a point never to conceal anything dutiable, and when his sons or the hired man accompanied him he told them in unmistakable terms that he would tolerate no dishonesty. And his reason for it was as

19

simple and unanswerable as everything about the man: It would bring God's blessing upon them.

As the years went by Arnold's love and respect for his father deepened. It could not but be otherwise. There was nothing his father demanded of him, or of his brother and sisters, that he did not first do himself. He wanted them to be industrious, and he labored more than all of them. If he corrected them it was never because of ill temper or tiredness. It was because he wanted them to be good, truly good. He had no material riches to give them, he wanted them to have the far greater riches of the spirit. In all his dealings with them he never gave way to anger or acted harshly. And he wanted them to act that way, too, not only among themselves, but with everyone they met. That line of behavior was founded on a principle that was deep in his heart. Many an evening when they were all gathered about him, he would expound that principle in simple words that were always filled with seriousness and always the same. "Children, whatever you do to your fellow men does not only affect them, it affects you too, be it good or evil. If you do good to your neighbor, it will hover over your head like a blessing; and if you do evil, it will hang about you like a curse. All that you do, you do in your own name, not in your father's or mother's; and for every good thing you do you will be blessed by God, for every evil thing you do you will be punished, here and hereafter."

It was his complete philosophy of life regarding his relations with other people. And when he voiced it the words would be filled with earnestness and emphasis. The things his father said always impressed Arnold deeply. They were never forgotten, because they were

20

lived out, realistically, in all their truth, before his eyes.

His father was a plain man, and Arnold unconsciously grew enamored of plainness. It became a symbol of greatness and truth. His father never appeared to be what he was not. He was real, true. He did not change. He cared for all of them, and he cast about the bitter, back-breaking grind of endless labor the romance of a great faith.

He had a formula for beginning his work, for facing a problem, for making a decision. It was a simple formula, made up of three words. "All with God." Sometimes he said it aloud, openly; for the most part it was just a dedication that welled up in his heart at the outset of any undertaking. And from the year long use of that little act of dedication there developed in him a deep-seated awareness that he did nothing alone or purely for himself. That awareness he carried into everything he did or said. When neighbors complained to him at times about the weather, what it was doing to their crops, and how they could do with more sunshine and less rain, he let them have their say. When they waited for his corroboration of their feelings on the matter, his quiet answer was not what they had expected. "It's all God's weather," he said simply, and the complainer was suddenly bereft of complaints.

The little parish church in Goch had an early Mass and a High Mass each Sunday. Gerard Janssen attended both of them and offered them up in honor of the Blessed Trinity, in thanksgiving for all graces and benefits received.

During Lent he used the family hour in the evening to read the epistle and gospel from the Mass of that day. Then he would turn with open pleasure to the

21

"Annals of the Propagation of the Faith." With great interest and warmth he would read from this publication the letters sent in by missionaries in foreign lands. When he was finished he would put down the periodical and he could not keep the enthusiasm and admiration out of his voice. "These are heroes, children," he would tell them, "heroes of the faith. They have given up everything for the good God." He would then go on to explain to them how men and women bound themselves by a triple vow to the religious life, and how, at a mere word from their superiors, they would be ready to go to the most distant countries to bring to the darkness of heathenism the light of faith.

And always in the intimacy of these family gatherings, Arnold would sit nearest to his father, all attention, all interest in everything that was said. At the outer edge of the glow cast by the fire sat his mother, quietly busy at her spinning wheel. She murmured something in a subdued sort of voice, and Arnold looked up at her. But she was completely absorbed, unaware of his gaze and of everyone else in the room. She had been praying, and, in the intensity of her recollection, a litle ejaculatory prayer had been spoken half aloud. The children were used to this. They called her their "praying mother," for she had the happy faculty of working busily and yet keeping her heart absorbed in prayer. They loved her for it, revered her, there was such an air of heavenly quiet always about her. But like the children they were they could not help teasing her at times about it. On Sundays she not only had the custom of going to the earliest Mass, but also of spending the greater part of the day in the church.

22

"Mother," the children would tease, "you are going to pray yourself clean through heaven."

She would look at them with gentle seriousness. "Can anyone tire of talking to the good God?" she would reply. Then looking at their bright young faces her look would deepen. "If one has eight children to take care of, one has to pray. What could I do without prayer? I must beg God and our Blessed Mother continuously to guard you against sin. I cannot guard my children alone."

The children would be silenced by her seriousness and the deep affection that underlay her words.

Arnold could recall so distinctly a certain day during the harvest season when he and his father, his brothers and sisters had to go out to the fields at the crack of dawn. His mother had been left all alone to do the housework. It was her custom never to miss Mass, and, in spite of all her work and household cares, she so arranged her time that she would get to church for Mass. His father knew what daily Mass meant to her and that she would have to miss it this day. Regretfully he told her that the work was so urgent with the harvesting that all the household chores must be done by her, and that left no time for Mass.

At lunch time his father glanced at the yard as he came in and noticed all the work had been done. He entered the house with the children and the noonday meal was ready. "Well, Mother," he said, "I see you got all the work done. I'm sorry you had to miss Mass, but there was no other way to arrange it."

"How can you talk that way, Gerard," she replied. "Do you think I could have gotten through all this work *without* going to Mass?"

He looked at her in complete surprise. "You went to Mass anyway?"

"Yes."

He looked about the room, swept and clean, the meal on the table, and he had seen the cattle in the pasture as he returned, and the other chores of the farmyard tended to. And she was not too well at the time. He turned on her a face soft with affection. "Yes, Anna, I don't think you could have gotten through all that work without going to Mass." He turned to the children. "Let us say grace now."

Arnold's mind was filled with the memory of that scene. Seated now by the side of his father he listened to that quiet voice as it went on and on in the warmth of the firelighted room. But he could not bring his mind to attend to what his father was saying. His gaze stayed fixed upon his mother. She sat there so simply and sweetly, unaware of all of them, her face so filled with peace and contentment that he knew what she had found was something ineffably true and good and priceless. He recalled the words his father had once spoken to him, about the similarity between him and his mother, and he wondered if his face ever showed, like hers now did, such a quiet placidity that was almost a joy.

Many a time he had gone with her after morning Mass, from station to station as she made the Way of the Cross; and her face then held that same rapt attention that it now held. It always produced in him a sense of quiet, of reverence, as though he had been admitted into the presence of something good and holy, as though he had been allowed to see one of her soul's deepest treasures, something she wanted to share with him. And he knew it was that way with all she had. She seemed to possess things only for others, for her children, for her neighbors, for the needy.

His attention came slowly back to his father. The assurance of that strong unpretentious voice brought a feeling of warmth and comfort. He felt himself folded in between two strong, loving arms, his mother with her gentle, continuous prayer, his father with his toil-hardened honesty of life and singleheartedness of view. Eveything was so simple and sure. Life just meant to do the work that God put into your hands to do — faithfully, prayerfully, with all your might. You are what you are, because that is all you are in His sight. What others might say or think of you was not impor-tant, what the good God thought of you, that was all-important. And He judged you by your heart, by the intention with which you did things. Life was as simple as all that. Knowing what He wants and doing it. If you did not know, you kept at what you were doing until He made clear to you what was His Will.

Chapter 4

WHEN OLD Father Lax died, Arnold became Mass server for one of the parish curates, Father Ruiter. The people of the parish looked on this priest as a saint. His charity knew no limits. He gave away his clothes and even his bed to the poor. One particularly cold winter he kept going about without an overcoat. His pastor finally noticed the fact and asked him for an explanation. A pastor is responsible for his curates, and while mortification is a good thing, self-inflicted pneumonia is suicide. He soon got to the bottom of Father Ruiter's strange behavior. There had been a very needy person and — he had given his overcoat away.

The pastor was touched by his curate's generosity. But being a pastor he had obligations to this young priest. So he gave him some kindly counsel on the virtue of prudence, and about the practical adage *"Primum vivere, deinde philosophizare,"* and as a climax to his fatherly admonitions he went out and bought a goodly bit of cloth for an overcoat. He gave it to Father Ruiter and told him to have one made in place of the one he had given away.

Father Ruiter thanked him sincerely, and went from the pastor's room with the bolt of cloth clutched in his arms.

For several days a fine, warm fatherly feeling filled the pastor's bosom. But the days stretched into a week and he suddenly observed that the new overcoat had not yet put in appearance. He summoned Father Ruiter and asked what was causing the delay. Humbly Father Ruiter began to make excuses. A horrible suspicion crowded up in the pastor's mind. Peremptorily, the pastor stood up and ordered him to appear before him within three days — with the overcoat. That ended poor Father Ruiter's attempts to explain.

On the day appointed he opened the pastor's room and walked in. The pastor looked up at him. "Well, where is the overcoat?"

Father Ruiter turned and gestured to several poor boys standing in the open doorway in back of him. They had on new suits. "They are wearing my overcoat, Father," he explained.

This was the priest for whom Arnold was now altar boy. Father Ruiter was soon interested in the boy. He loaned him books, mostly of a devotional nature, he talked with him about them, he became the boy's confidant. The words and actions of the priest made a lasting impression on the boy.

When Arnold was about ten years old a preparatory school was opened in the town. Father Ruiter knew of the boy's desire to study, so he went to Arnold's parents and asked them to enroll Arnold in the school. Arnold's father shook his head regretfully in refusal. The expense of the boy's schooling would be too much for them to meet. They wanted Arnold to help them with the farm. He was the oldest boy; they would need him behind the plough.

Father Ruiter made no attempt to answer any of these objections. They were all valid. He knew that. Instead he began speaking to the boy's father about the kindly and wondrous care exercised by Providence over all earthly creatures, about the way the good God clothed the flowers of the field with breathtaking beauty, and how He cared for the birds of the air and the beasts of the field. Would He not be as solicitous for the earthly needs of men? He was qualified to speak. He had lived out this belief in God's all-providing care before the eyes of all the people of the village.

Gerard Janssen listened gravely, humbly to the words of the priest, and when he had finished he made no attempt to defend his former attitude. He quietly gave his consent for his boy to go to school.

On the second day of January Arnold entered the preparatory school. From the outset it was evident that he liked to study, but things did not come to him easily. His was not the type of mind that leaps quickly to the understanding of a new thought or a foreign language. It was the slower, more searching sort of intellect, that comes to its knowledge by careful inquiry, and then clings tenaciously to the truths it has found. He worked hard and his school reports were consistently good.

But his career at the preparatory school in his native town was short-lived. The following year a diocesan college for resident students was opened in the town of Gaesdonck, on the Dutch border. It was only a few miles distant and Arnold transferred to this school. The curriculum of studies at this new school was a rather diversified one, since it was the aim of the college to prepare students not only for theological studies but also for any of the other professions.

The Rector of the College, Father Perger, was a very capable man, who combined thorough knowledge and practicality with solid piety and kindliness of heart.

Under this man's guidance Arnold spent the next six years of his life. The boy was talented, but no juvenile prodigy. He did have two qualities, however, that were outstanding: remarkable diligence and thoroughness. None of his fellow pupils could match his painstaking care and industry.

The course of studies carried the usual assortment of languages and scientific studies. He applied himself faithfully to all the subjects allotted him, but from the outset it was apparent that Arnold had a decided flair for mathematics. His classmates soon discovered that fact, and when a tough problem had them in despair they would inevitably have recourse to him.

It was no uncommon occurrence for a group of them to gather about him in the study hall and silently wait for him to unravel the complexities of some problem that had them all at their wit's end.

Oblivious of all those standing about him, his pencil would move swiftly over the paper putting down cryptic symbols, and all the while the thumb and index finger of his left hand twisted and tugged at a lock of hair above his left temple.

"Look at that," one of the onlookers whispered nudging his neighbor, "look at that, will you?"

"Look at what?"

"That." He pointed to the left thumb and finger busy at their task. "Arnold's going to twist the solution out of that lock of hair again."

And eventually Arnold would look up at them with satisfaction in his quiet eyes, and give them the answer.

The Christmas, Easter and summer vacations were spent at home, but Arnold had grown so enamored of his books that he spent most of these vacation days in studying. His presence brought a new element into the uneventful placidity of the family evening hour. He had to share with them the new things he had learned, the amazing wonders of science and the stirring events of history. It was like a fresh new current thrusting its invigorating strength into an old, slow-moving stream.

One night he told them in detail the sufferings and persecution that the Catholics of Ireland were going through, and he spoke so warmly and vividly that all of them were deeply moved. His father, with his usual practicality, at once decided to do something about the matter. "From tonight on," he announced, "we are going to add an Our Father to our night prayers, for poor, distressed Ireland."

The talk then moved on to other things, and when time came for night prayers it was William's turn to lead. He was Arnold's third brother, and a source of worry at times to both parents. He had a gay, lively disposition, and would strike up a ready acquaintance with anybody and everybody. More than once his mother had cautioned him that: "Friendship makes and unmakes you." She had in fact a regular little armory of old maxims which she used on him and his failings. He had a generous view of things, so he thought, and was inclined to let little matters take care of themselves. Repeatedly she warned him: "He who does not pay attention to small things will never enjoy great ones." And when he skimped his work she told him that "A lazy man is a pillow on which the devil loves to rest."

She noticed that William would always take her admonitions in good part, but there was a doubt whether the seriousness of her words had made as deep an impression on him as she wished. More than any of the others he would give way to drowsiness at prayer time. How many times he had been sent to kneel by his father's side so that he would not sleep through his night prayers. But she loved him for his sunny disposition, and his surprising evidences, on unexpected occasions, that the things she had admonished him about had been after all remembered.

He started the beads and went through them perfectly. Then came the litany. When it was finished they all waited for their father's voice to begin the solemn prayer: "In the beginning was the Word..." But he said nothing. One by one they turned and looked at him. He was gazing steadily, almost sternly at William. William looked back at him, wondering what on earth he had done wrong now. His father's voice broke the silence: "One Our Father for Ireland."

Confusion reddened William's face at having so quickly forgotten. Quickly he started the prayer and they all joined in. No one forgot the one Our Father for Ireland from that day on.

It bothered William to see Arnold so completely wrapped up in his books. It completely warred with his idea of what a vacation should be. Besides Arnold was rather puny and all this book work was not good

31

for him. He tried repeatedly to coax him away from them. On one occasion, by appealing to his ever-ready spirit of helpfulness, he succeeded.

Arnold was bent studiously over his books, and William, dressed in his working clothes, had watched him for several minutes. "Arnold," he finally said, "it's going to be very hot out in the fields today."

Arnold looked up. "Yes, it will be, Willy. It's warm even in here."

"Our sandwiches will be as dry as wood shavings by lunch time. Couldn't you play the prophet Habakkuk for us today, and bring our meal to us?"

Arnold smiled. "Gladly, Willy. I'll bring it," he promised.

At midday he brought his brothers their lunch. As they ate they began to tease him about his ability with books and his inability to plough. They challenged him to turn a furrow. Nothing daunted, he took the handles of the plough and started the team forward. The plough twisted and turned as though it were possessed of a will of its own. Manfully he held on, trying to subdue the recalcitrant jerks and swervings of that sharp-edged slippery ploughshare. He fought the thing all the way down to the edge of the field and back again. Triumphantly he looked at his brothers, and then wiped the sweat that poured down his pale face.

His brothers grouped themselves about him, silently surveying the furrow he had ploughed. They said nothing. They only stood and looked. He turned and followed their gaze. Two furrows wandered wildly and drunkenly across the field.

"Yes, sir," judged William, "that is what I call a furrow." His brothers nodded their heads gravely. "You know something, Arnold; you are wasting your time with books. You're a born farmer. Look at that!" His hand cut a serpentine gesture in the air indicating the course of the furrow, and the whole group was suddenly convulsed with laughter.

When Arnold could speak, he assured them that he appreciated their advice but would not follow it. The straight answer to a mathematical problem was his meat. He would have to leave straight furrows to them. Smilingly he went back to his books.

There was a famous shrine of Our Lady in the town of Kevelaer, a good two hours' walk distant from Arnold's town. Arnold wanted to make a pilgrimage to the shrine and had small difficulty in interesting William in the idea. Their parents readily gave their consent and early one morning the two youthful pilgrims set forth.

They had hardly gotten clear of the Stone Gate which marked the entrance to the town when Arnold began to pray aloud. William looked at him in amazement. He was startled, not by the praying, but by the quiet assurance, the lack of self-consciousness, and the place. It was right here that his father had done the same thing a few days ago. They were going to haul some salt to Nymwegen and his father was on the first wagon and he on the second. It was the dark of early morning and his father had halted his wagon and said: "William, it is still dark and no one can see us. Take out your beads and walk by the side of your horse; I will do the same. We shall pray until it gets light; in order that the Lord may protect us today against sin

33

and misfortune." It had impressed him, and here was Arnold doing the same thing, but with no explanations, and no concern about being seen. And the prayer kept up the whole way. An uncle of theirs lived in one of the hamlets through which they passed, but Arnold did not stop for a visit. Willie had visioned the trip as an excursion, but Arnold evidently meant the real thing when he talked about a pilgrimage.

At Kevelaer they went to confession and communion and made a long thanksgiving. By that time it was noon, and they were still fasting. Arnold got out some money and told William to buy their favorite delicacy — apple dumplings.

William bought six of the largest he could find and the two boys sat down behind a pile of lumber and ate dumplings. Arnold looked at his brother. "You still hungry, Willy?"

"I could eat some more — if I had them."

Arnold brought out some money. "Get some more then."

William got three more and Arnold gave him two and kept one for himself.

When the last crumb had disappeared they went back to pray again at the shrine, and then started homeward. They walked, praying the entire way.

That night they told the rest of the family all about their pilgrimage, William doing most of the talking. Arnold had little to say about the trip, and nothing about the impressions made upon him or what stirrings of grace he had felt while kneeling in prayer at the shrine. But the pilgrimage had filled some deep need in his heart, for, from that time forward, he unfailingly made a pilgrimage during his vacation time to the shrine of Our Lady at Kevelaer.

His incessant attention to his books, however, began to become a matter of some concern to his mother. He had never been robust, and she feared that his ceaseless application to his studies might completely undermine his health. Her married sister, Elizabeth, lived in a nearby town, and had a rollicking brood of five small sons. She decided to send Arnold to her on a visit, hoping that the companionship of his cousins would draw him away from his books.

The five lively boys readily accepted the little bookworm into their congenial company, and soon had him running all over the countryside with them. They had vivid imaginations, and a stick made a rifle and a clump of bushes a bear. Ruddy of cheek and bright of eye they would return home to recount to their mother the enormous animals they had encountered and slain on their sham hunting expeditions. When they had finished their extravagant recital Aunt Elizabeth would turn to the quiet-eyed, smiling Arnold and ask him what deeds of prowess he had done. But before he could reply the others broke in protectively, informing their mother that he was not supposed to *do* things; he was a student, a professor, who read books and gave lessons and speeches. And then they turned on him and asked him to go ahead and show their mother, make a speech for her. And so Arnold gave them a small speech, to the complete satisfaction and amusement of all present. The boys were delighted and made it a point of pride, on every possible occasion, to ask Arnold to give a speech. And when Arnold saw that the older folks wanted it, he would give them a little speech.

The stay with his relatives did wonders for him and he went back to school a much healthier looking youngster.

It was an established custom among the farmfolk of that region that when a boy was able to sow he should be allowed to smoke. That memorable event was usually fixed for a boy's sixteenth birthday. It marked the transition from boyhood to young manhood. When Arnold had attained his sixteenth year he, too, was granted his long pipe, and seemed to enjoy not only the use of the pipe but the sense of maturity that it was a sign of. At the same time his father gave both him and his brothers the attitude they should have toward drinking. His father was no teetotaler, but he was abstemious in the use of alcoholic drinks. He cautioned them about using beer and wines temperately, and his sane attitude was readily understood by the boys and obeyed. He gave each of them a moderate allowance for pocket money. It was enough for their individual needs and small pleasures. "Parents who give their children too much money," he was wont to say, "so that they can take part in everything and show off, only make them unhappy."

The years of Arnold's schooling went swiftly by and the family which had shared so intimately with him all the ups and downs of these student years was not excluded from the momentous final event. He wrote to his parents: "Next week we shall be taken to Muenster for our examinations. Pray hard!"

His mother did not need this reminder. Every morning, during that time, her first question after returning from Mass would be: "No letter from Arnold yet?"

At long last his letter came. "There were eleven of

us at the examinations. All went well. I had had trouble in acquiring a good Latin style, so to improve it I learned Cicero's speech *Pro Lege Manilia* by heart. It did the trick. I passed the examinations!"

On July 11, 1855, Arnold graduated from college. He was now eighteen years old and when he returned to Goch he told his parents that he wanted to study theology in order to become a priest. His father and mother in their quiet prayerful way thought over the idea, and then calmly and gladly gave their consent.

Less than two years after Arnold had started school, Father Ruiter died. The helping of his little altar boy toward obtaining an education was just another one of the kind deeds that fills the life of a busy, zealous, good priest, be he pastor or curate. But this random good deed had strangely wide results, and whenever the achievements of Arnold Janssen are spoken of, there, too, will be mentioned the name of the young curate who, under God, was responsible for their start.

Chapter 5

I N OCTOBER, 1855, Arnold entered the Collegium Borromaeum, at Muenster. This was an ecclesiastical seminary but the students attended classes in Philosophy and Theology at the Academy of Muenster, a State school which, later on, became a university.

The courses in philosophy required also a number of credits in various sciences, and that fact afforded Arnold the opportunity to pursue more extensively his interest in the natural sciences. He attended all the lectures on physics and chemistry, botany and zoology, but was handicapped by his inability to buy all the needed books.

He knew the burden under which his father labored in providing for the family, and he had determined from the start of his schooling that he would cut all personal expenses to the bone. The farm gave his family a living, but ready cash was always a scarce item. For that reason he had made an arrangement with his

Bishop whereby he would pay the cost of his studies later on, from his salary, when he was a priest.

His predilection for mathematics found full scope in this new school and he delved deeply into it. He began speculating about a new theory of numbers, and when the theory was sufficiently thought out he presented the idea to Father Perger, who had quite a name as a mathematician. Father Perger did not offer an opinion about the scientific soundness of the project, its feasibility or its possibilities. He merely expressed the suspicion that there might be intellectual pride at the bottom of the whole thing. Arnold dropped his new theory of numbers like a hot potato.

He was only 19 years old when he completed his course of philosophy, and that was three years too young for admission to theological studies.

Bishop Mueller of Muenster suggested that he attend the University of Bonn and do some further studies toward obtaining a diploma for college teaching. Qualified teachers were needed by the diocese and the government required the *facultas docendi* from a state school before allowing any one to function as a teacher.

The suggestion appealed to Arnold and he at once made a trip home to lay the plan before his parents. His father opposed it. The old objection was still there — lack of funds — but that was not the main trouble. There were too many dangers for a young man in a big city like Bonn. He could not reconcile himself to the thought of Arnold being so far from the family, living alone, in the midst of so many incitements to evil.

Arnold tried, without minimizing the dangers of city life, to assure his father that he would use all the safe-

4

guards and care possible, but his words were unable to budge his father from the stand he had taken. The University of Bonn seemed to fade away into the distance — a far-off distance — a distance of three years. Things looked rather hopeless for the eager young student, when help arrived from an unexpected source.

There was a college acquaintance of Arnold's by the name of Weghmann who lived in Goch. He was several years older than Arnold and was home on a vacation from the University. He met Arnold and heard all about the abrupt ending of his hopes for further studies. Weghmann was studying law and the inflexibility of Arnold's father acted on him like a challenge. He offered to help Arnold out of his predicament by having a talk with his father, and Arnold gratefully accepted.

With cool aplomb Weghmann bearded the lion in his den. He bombarded the sturdy old man with facts and figures about city life, with exhortations and eulogies about Arnold, until the simple old man could find no answers any more, and completely succumbed. The budding lawyer had won his first case.

Arnold was happy at his father's capitulation, and the whole family with him, especially his mother. She knew her boy, and she had no fear that in the big city his ideals would suffer. She felt that his vocation was secure. All that it needed was more prayer, and she would tend to that.

At Bonn a completely new life began for Arnold. He had not minded too much his years away from home at prep school or college. In both these places there had been an intimate warm little circle made up by teachers and pupils that had been a wider and larger replica of the intimate little circle at home. But here everything was different. Everyone went their own way, unconcerned what others did, untouched by their efforts, their failures or success.

He rented a little room, and had to take care of all his needs. It was lonely at first, and the letters from home were small warm events in a large cold world. He was just one small cipher in the large busy world of the University.

And then one day he met a student by the name of Lamers. They had been classmates in prep school, and the meeting was for him an event. They joined forces, became fast friends. The faith which had made of their prep school days such a heart-warming memory, became again the basis for a new and deeper relationship. Every morning they went to Mass together, and every two weeks they went to the sacraments. Both of them joined the Sodality, and when Lamers was elected prefect Arnold rejoiced as though he himself had won the responsible post.

The first four terms at the University Arnold devoted almost entirely to the natural sciences, and succeeded on one occasion in winning a prize for an essay on a botanical subject.

In the summer of 1858 a competition was announced for a mathematical essay on curves. The award was to be a financial one, fifty thalers. Arnold entered the competition and won it. His essay was so well done that the University accepted it, also, in place of the usual written examination paper for securing the *facultas docendi* (the certificate for teaching).

The public press carried a little news story about the competition and the young man who had won it. When

41

some of the neighbors came storming into the Janssen household waving newspapers in their hands and shouting congratulations the family was overwhelmed. They just could not believe that their quiet Arnold had done this remarkable thing.

In the meanwhile Arnold, with fifty shining thalers in his pocket, had only one shining idea in his head: to repay in a small measure all the sacrifices his father had made for him. He sat down and wrote a letter, asking his father to come and visit him in Bonn. The prize money would take care of all the expenses.

It is not hard to imagine what serious deliberation the old man gave to the project before finally consenting.

The long railroad trip to Bonn was for him a trip around the world. He had never covered such a distance, never seen so much. In Cologne he viewed the glories of its incomparable cathedral. In the city of Bonn, with his boy at his side, he walked confusedly through the bustle and clang of city life. For several days he went about in that place of huge buildings and hurrying people, like a man in a dream. The short trip on the Rhine up to Remagen was a blessed relief. And then the journey home.

He came back again to the little town of Goch, to the age-old house with the curry comb on the sign before it, to the drudgery of farming and the monotony of trucking loads of salt, to his plough and his team of horses. He had seen the world. Cathedrals and cities were good, but the simplicity of his native place was better. They were wonderful places but they had nothing more in the last analysis than Goch. Work and prayer were all that any job offered, that any city could offer a man. And he had seen how in the great places of the earth work could be wedded not to prayer but to pleasure. It was better here, in the little town, on the Street of Our Lady. There was peace and less hurrying, and men went further.

Arnold had spent every cent of his prize money but he had bought a great thing with it. The memory of that trip he knew would be for his aging father one of the most memorable events in all of his steady going life. The joy and wonder of that journey would be food for thought and talk for many a month to come.

With empty pockets but a happy heart, Arnold went back to the humdrum of university life. There was no longer the original loneliness of his first days at the University to haunt him. He had a goodly number of acquaintances now who would drop in on him at odd times for a friendly pipe or a bit of companionship. But it was a very casual, loosely-knit sort of group that these acquaintances made. There was not the help and encouragement that came from a closely-knit family circle, and he wanted them to draw more closely to each other, see more of each other for the mutual help and advantage of all.

He gathered them all together at last and succeeded in forming them into a little club. It was quite a satisfaction to have succeeded in this first step. Arnold had some rather high-minded plans for all of them, but he would broach them gradually.

Their first corporate act was to be an all day hike. It started out beautifully, all of them in high spirits. But it ended on a different note. At a wayside inn the entire club looked too long upon the wine while it was red and as a result not only lost the focusing power of their eyes but also the locomotive power of their limbs.

Sober Arnold had to hire a wagon, load the convivial delinquents into it, and cart the sodden club back to the University.

Disillusioned, he dissolved the club, and shortly after that he gave up his one little luxury of smoking. Nobody could prevail upon him from that time forward, even during vacation time, to light a pipe or cigar.

In June, 1859, Arnold took an examination in mathematics, physics, mineralogy, botany, zoology and chemistry, and came off with flying colors. His name and qualifications for professorship was published by the University and he had an immediate offer to teach in Berlin at an attractive salary. He was twenty-two years of age, the salary offered was excellent, the place a decided inducement, the capital city of the country, one of the largest metropolises of Europe. Without a moment's hesitation Arnold turned down the proposition. It was not what he was aiming at. His mind was firmly set on being a priest.

His decision, to all his acquaintances, was incomprehensible. He had fitted himself to be a teacher of the sciences, and he was now equipped to be one. The first offer, and a very alluring one, he turns down. Why? Because he wanted to be a priest. If that had been at the back of his mind all the time why had he been studying natural sciences? A certain amount of them is good and useful, but for a prospective priest the sacred sciences should have been his specialty. There was no sense in his behavior.

Yet Arnold's thought was completely logical, and

44

the answer to his seemingly contradictory behavior was, like the young man himself, very simple.

He had a natural bent for the sciences, but his personal preference had no part in the matter. It was a different motive that moved him. At that particular period many scientists, captivated by the apparent success of the Darwinian theory, had begun with renewed zeal to forge weapons against the fundamentals of Christianity. Quite a few Catholics, deluded by specious attacks, had lost their faith, many others were torn by doubts.

He considered it timely and important to meet this new enemy on its own grounds, to fight fire with fire. He felt that only Catholic men, trained along scientific lines, could successfully fight the pseudo-science of this new irreligion. And at the same time he felt that genuine science would act as a revelation of God and of His glories in creation. For to him "the vital force, which in plants and animals, forms such a variety of organs both highly suitable and beautiful, and with astonishing constancy continues to transmit remarkable instincts and tendencies from generation to generation" was a manifestation of God's wisdom and greatness and beauty. To declare that to the world of irreligion was the task of religion. It was the function of the Church to lift the world from its worship of nature to the worship of the supernatural. And the priest was the representative of the Church.

It was all strictly coherent. He judged that for the present day and age a priest needed not only the sacred sciences but also a rather comprehensive view of the natural sciences. But the sacred sciences were, of course, the most needful for the priest.

45

He took another term of work at the University, devoting almost all of his time now to theology.

In the autumn of 1859 he went back to Muenster and entered the seminary as a student in the second theological course. He had only one year in which to prepare for the final examination and then another year of preparation for ordination.

He went at this last period of preparation with his usual absorption, and the unanimous opinion of his professors was that this was a candidate for the priesthood who was "uncommonly diligent and attentive."

Chapter 6

$\mathcal{T}$HROUGH ALL his student years Arnold wrote frequently and faithfully to his family. The shyness, the reticence that characterized him, for the most part, in his dealings with others, gave way to complete frankness and ready expression when he spoke or wrote to his own relatives. It was as though he knew there would be no misunderstanding of his motives, no ridicule of his devotion and ideals, for the warmth of the same faith bound them together, the oneness of years of prayer and work together, and the seeking of the same ultimate goal.

He was in the final months of his preparation for the priesthood when he wrote a letter to his mother. It was intended to reach her on the feast-day of her patron saint. It is a revealing letter, opening up the thoughts of his mind and the sentiments of his heart on the great event so long looked forward to and prepared for, and now so soon to be realized.

47

"Dearly beloved mother:

I am sitting alone in my little room, in the early morning light. At my side the candle is burning, while in front of me stands a picture of Christ; and all is peaceful, very peaceful in my soul. From a distant steeple the sound of a bell comes to me, summoning the faithful to rise from their sleep, and go to church, where the holy sacrifice is about to be offered. It affects me deeply when I think that soon I, too, shall step up to the altar, stand there in place of Jesus Christ, and celebrate the sacred mysteries. And then my thoughts turn back to the past years of my life, to the days of my childhood and the days of my youth at home, to the way you cared for me and guided me. I recall how you encouraged me to do good, and how, when I was away from home, you did not cease to pray daily for me, to the Giver of all good things. I still recall the happy hour when first I learned that you were willing to grant my heart's desire. The years of study, with their labors and trials, stand before me. And now I am close to the goal. In a year I may be active as a priest.

And reflecting seriously on all this, I know that I owe many thanks to God for His fatherly guidance. He has given me success in all my efforts. He has preserved me from sickness and great misfortune. In the dangers that have accompanied my studies, His hand has not allowed me to stray."

There were additional words of congratulation on her feast day, and wishes that her health and happiness might be preserved to the family for many years to come, and there was a humble request that she keep him always in her prayers.

The respect and reverence which all of his family had for the priesthood had been part of Arnold's own make-up, too. And the example of priests like Father Ruiter and Father Perger had deepened that attitude, and had made of it something to be prized above all earthly attainments. But he was still a very young man, and it is strange to see in one so young so deep an awareness of the road he had travelled, so sober a reviewing of the dangers encountered, so grateful a counting of the help and favors received.

The shining brightness of what stands before is usually wont to so entrance the eyes of the seeker that the pain and labor of those who had made his success possible is easily forgotten. But there was in Arnold always this deep spirit of gratefulness to the human agents of his success, and to the Divine Goodness that had used these agents to bless his efforts.

And as the months went by and the day of ordination drew closer that gratitude deepened and with it other feelings. In a letter that he wrote to his parents a week before his ordination there is a presentiment of things to come: "Rejoice with me," he wrote, "and praise the Lord who has done great things to me, who has guided me so lovingly, and who, in a few days, will show me His kindness in a still greater measure. Pray for me that the Lord may make of me a worthy priest. *It may be that His hand is already extended to give me, along with the reception of Holy Orders, great graces, and He is only waiting, perhaps, for you to ask Him for them.* The Lord is about to furnish me with a means that will enable me to recompense you for all your sacrifices on my behalf. I shall remember you in my first Mass."

He was fully aware, of course, that his ordination would bring with it the graces of the priesthood. His feeling that the Hand of God "might already be extended to give him great graces" indicates, for the first time, a vague sense that God might want great deeds of him. And it is noteworthy that he humbly refers the possibility of these graces being granted to the prayers of others, to the prayers of his praying mother, his stalwart father, and that home circle of working, believing brothers and sisters who made up the family from which he came.

He was not quite 24 years old when Bishop John G. Mueller ordained him. His first Mass he celebrated in the parish church at Goch, quietly, on a weekday, for it was not then the custom to add much pomp and ceremony to a first Mass.

But for Arnold it was the day of days. He was a priest. His goal had been achieved, and it had been achieved by work and prayer, the way his father had taught him to achieve anything in life. He was now a priest, an unassuming, frail-bodied, pious priest who, by dint of perseverance, had reached the goal on which his heart was set. That was the way most people thought of him, that was the way his own friends in the seminary and clerical circles regarded him. He had acquired an extraordinary amount of scientific knowledge, but no one seemed to hold that as of any importance. It had no significance. Perhaps because he never paraded it. A visiting Bishop gave the general estimate of him in one sentence. "He'll probably do as a curate."

But his own Bishop had no plans like that for Arnold

Janssen. Soon after ordination he was appointed professor and assistant rector at the newly established high school at Bocholt. He struck up an immediate and lasting friendship with the Rector, Father Waldau, who was considerably older than he.

Two small benefices at the parish church were assigned Father Janssen to provide him with some sort of salary. As the holder of these benefices he had pastoral duties to discharge, hearing of confession on week ends and Mass and preaching on Sundays and holidays. He was zealous, punctual and energetic in the discharge of these duties.

The only weak point in his priestly activities was his singing. On one occasion he was asked to sing a High Mass at the town of Dingden. The preparation far outdid the performance. He had practiced faithfully for the event but when he sang the Mass a strange thing came to pass. He stood at the altar, the missal open before him, and his head moved up and down according as the notes on the musical score indicated a rise or fall in pitch, but his voice came forth a strange untuneful sameness. He wrote about the event. "I never celebrated High Mass while at Bocholt. Only once in Dingden did I venture to sing it. But so many unflattering remarks were made that I gave up all further attempts." He became one of the perpetual subdeacons for High Masses. A subdeacon does not have to be a skylark, he just has to be useful.

After several years the school had so expanded that it was transferred to a new building. Father Janssen's teaching work kept on increasing until he was handling twenty-four classes a week, and those classes covered practically all branches of study. Eventually additional teachers were engaged, and some of his burden of work lightened. His main branch was mathematics, and along with that he taught business accounting, the natural sciences and French.

His students were fascinated by him, not only because his knowledge was wide and deep, but because he could present it in an interesting way. Over and above that he had an affection for them that was deep and real, and it showed itself in many ways but especially in his complete devotion to the obligations he had as their teacher. Teaching was to him a very responsible calling. It did not merely consist in carefully preparing his classes and painstakingly correcting four to five sets of written lessons each week. To his mind the true purpose of his work, was to lead forth the young minds entrusted to him into knowledge and the young souls into truth. He wanted to educate both the head and the heart.

There is a letter of his Rector, Father Waldau, about this matter, which gives a very clear picture of the young priest as an educator. "His manner of teaching proved that he had thoroughly digested and mastered his subjects; he prepared very carefully for every class and took great pains to make the matter in hand as plain as possible to his students. He also knew how to encourage them in their home work. He corrected their written work very conscientiously, and the results obtained deserve the highest praise. He devoted special efforts to securing equipment for his physics class and specimens for his natural science work. He was an excellent disciplinarian. Not only in school, but also outside, he made great efforts to raise and keep up a high standard in morals and religion among his students. His exemplary conduct won the esteem of all."

His seriousness was too much a part of him, his sincerity too whole-hearted not to have gained the respect of all. It was part of the man, part of that life he had lived as a boy on the farm. There he had not only seen but had been a sharer in the hard work that had to be faced relentlessly and carried uncomplainingly in order to wrest from the soil a meager living. But he had not derived from all that the grim bitter outlook that life was merely a round of toil that had to be stoically born if one would live. The deep faith of his parents ran like a thread of light through the dark weave of unending toil. Work, their work, the work allotted to their hands, their particular position in life was the will of a loving God. Everything connected with life had to be done carefully, thoroughly, unsparing of tiredness and time, for it was done for Him. And somehow that attitude lifted the curse from work and made of it a blessing. Life was a wonderful arena in which each one proved himself, proved his love by eager going forth to labor, and by glad acceptance of it, and even seeking more of it.

His attitude toward his students was the same he would have had if they were so many younger brothers of his working on his father's farm. It was more on the serious than the indulgent side. One did not learn industry through indulgence. He could remember his father's and mother's example of seriousness and work, and he knew that through the lessons he had learned from them he had come to the position he now held. He could only give to these boys the good that he had learned, the good that he knew to be good from

53

experience in other schools and colleges and the university.

Both in work and self-discipline he made great demands upon himself, and he expected his students to do the same. He led them, they did not lead him, and they looked up to him with wholesome respect. But he was not a heartless taskmaster. He knew very well how to let down the bars, how to smile, and enter into their simple games and joys at the right time. We catch a glance of that in a letter he wrote home in June of 1866. "Today we went on an excursion with our students. They had three trumpets, a sabre for the commander, two drums. (The big one we loaned from the burgomaster.) At the head of the band of marchers one of the boys carried a beautiful black, red and golden flag. We left at half-past one in the afternoon. First we played 'cops and robbers'; then we had refreshments. Afterwards, the boys tootled around for a while on their trumpets and made a din with the drums; then came a game of blind man's bluff, and we ended with a return to 'cops and robbers.' At the very last, I, as a solitary policeman, had the misfortune to be captured by a large number of robbers under the chieftainship of the Rector, Father Waldau."

Whatever Arnold did, he did thoroughly, and one can well imagine that he was wholeheartedly a sharer in such simple recreations. It is no wonder that his twelve years of labor there were regarded by all his associates as years of perfect peace and contentment for him. He seemed so content with little things, with the steady satisfaction of classwork and school routine and with the busy week ends of pastoral work.

But very few, if any of them, had an intimation of

54

what was going on in the young priest's soul. It is true his fellow teachers observed that he had the custom of making the stations of the cross several times a day, and that he had talked the Rector into having fifteen minutes of spiritual reading during dinner; but they were not aware of his steadily growing desire for a full and complete surrender to the arms of Divine Love. That fact he confided only to his parents. "We must," he wrote in one of his letters, "offer ourselves to God, as Mary did, with childlike confidence, and ask Him to deal with us according to His holy Will; we must not lavish our affections on the things of this world, but direct them to God, our supreme good, who wants our *whole heart.*"

He wrote that in 1865. It was not just the effusion of a prayerful moment. Like all his thoughts and actions it was the result of close, quiet consideration. It was a treasure that he had discovered, and at once he shared it with the ones to whom he owed so much. Having shared it with them, he went ahead and lived it. For a number of years, he went about doing the duties of his daily life, imbuing all the hours of the day with the simple thought he had discovered; directing his heart to God, offering himself with childlike confidence to God, asking Him to deal with him according to His Will.

The upshot of those years of quiet prayer and ceaseless work was a resolution which he put down on paper, in Latin, in the year 1871.

At first glance, it seems something of no great importance, except possibly to him and his pious designs. The gist of the whole resolution was that he had determined to say Mass without a stipend, on all Fridays

5

of the year, in order to honor the Sacred Heart, and to pay homage to the Holy Trinity, dwelling in that Sacred Heart.

It is a lengthy document, and seems to be much ado about very little. He lists numerically all his reasons for this little resolution, like the steps in the solution of a problem: "First, that the Triune God, through the superabundance of graces in the most Sacred Heart, may increase prayers and good works, as well as the number of believers throughout the world; secondly, that He may bless the prayers, labors, and sufferings of all the faithful, but especially of those souls who are privileged by Him to gain merits for his Church; thirdly, that He, our High Priest and Lover of souls, may unite us more closely with His Sacred Heart and enrich with greater graces *all those priests who adopt this holy practice.*"

The last line comes as a surprise. This was not just a resolution; it was a plan, directed toward other priests.

It is a bit out of the ordinary to find a young priest, in a remote boy's school, concerned about arousing the interest of priests in such a purely spiritual project. But it is even more out of the ordinary to see him putting his plan down, so lengthily, in the formalized phrases of the Latin language, as though it were some kind of solemn pronouncement or official manifesto. And strangest of all is the fact that on closer reading the three reasons proposed on the document begin to take on the proportions of something more than just pious-sounding effusions. This young man is concerned very intimately with the affairs of God. He wants all the vast desires of Christ's heart to be fulfilled. In effect he is asking that there be a spread of faith,

56

and a deepening of faith, and that the ones who work for that twofold aim (the priests who offer Mass on Fridays for that intention) may be drawn into a deeper love and closer union with their Divine High Priest.

Through the simple words there breathes an apostolic faith that does not limit the enterprise to any country or continent. There is in it the worldwide scope that characterizes the vast desires of the Sacred Heart. Something great was stirring in the soul of Father Janssen and he was so filled with the truth and goodness of it that he was eager to impart it to others, to have them see the vast vision that he saw, to have them share their blessings with others as yet unblessed.

One begins to wonder about this young priest and his quiet years of contentment. Perhaps the twelve uneventful years of routine work before a blackboard, the treadmill plodding back and forth from room to chapel, from chapel to classroom, from school to parish church and from parish church back to school again, perhaps these were not such uneventful years as they seemed to be. The placid face, the alert eyes, the disciplined ways of speech, the quiet smile may have concealed a soul that had in it anything but the sameness of the ordinary. These years of quiet work and prayer may have been a time of great growth and soul stress, for where there are banked up fires of desire the denial of those desires for expression can only cause the flames to burn more deeply and intensely. The vision of vast achievements to be accomplished, of heights to be reached, can turn ordinary work and tasks into grinding slavery. An eagle will fly, and a cage will kill it. The far-flung reaches of the sky are its domain, and if bound to the earth it dies. But Father Arnold was no eagle. He would have laughed embarrassingly at the very thought of such a comparison. He knew his domain. Preaching and confessions on week ends, the daily care and teaching of his boys. He had great desires. Every true priest has those. A priest is, like His Master, a man of desires, great desires, the desires of Christ's heart. And for them he must pray and sacrifice and do the work entrusted to his hands. Each one in his own allotted place. He was just a priest who had no fear of work in any shape or form, who loved to pray, and who had desires, large desires, that somehow included others, many others beside himself. But they were only desires, and the only way he could see to put them into effect was through this resolution so carefully thought out and written down in Latin.

But the resolution had no success. The practice he had conceived for enlisting other priests in this apostolic crusade did not spread. Few, if any, seemed to feel as he did about the whole matter. There was nothing novel or particularly attractive about the idea. It was just a simple pious idea of a simple pious man. It was his — all his.

Chapter 7

*T*HE SUMMER vacation of 1867 Father Janssen spent in traveling. He first went to the Industrial Exposition at Paris and then made a visit to the grave of St. Jeane Baptist Marie Vianney, the Cure d'Ars, for whom he had a special veneration. From there he went to Innsbruck to attend the General Convention of German Catholics. It was here that he met Father Malfatti, S. J., the Director for Germany and Austria-Hungary of the Apostleship of Prayer.

The members of the Apostleship of Prayer worked for the glory of God and the salvation of souls by uniting all their prayers, labors and sufferings, with those of the Sacred Heart. That apostolic purpose, and the fact that the members cultivated a special devotion to the Sacred Heart made a strong appeal to Father Janssen. When Father Malfatti suggested that he take over the propagation and direction of the Apostleship for the diocese of Muenster, Father Janssen readily accepted, and his Bishop officially placed him in charge of the work.

59

Energetically, he took up his new duties. He was still a professor at the boy's school of Bocholt and his class-work and professional duties remained his first concern. But whenever he could find an opportunity he went from parish to parish, on foot, to propagate the Apostle-ship of Prayer. His vacations offered him a better chance for this work, and he used every one of them for that purpose. The summer vacations, the mid-term holidays, the Easter and Christmas holidays became for the young priest apostolic journeys. From parish to parish he plodded, arousing the spirit of apostolic prayer, speaking to group after group about the sufferings and setbacks of the Church in her world-wide aspirations for the saving of souls, exhorting the faithful to widen their hearts, to be generous with the generosity of the Sacred Heart.

He loved every moment of the work; its trials and tiredness seemed to mean nothing to him. This was the kind of work the Apostles had done, bringing the light of the Word to a world that had grown so care-less it was living in darkness.

The aims of this crusade were so simple and practical that it was easy for him to speak enthusiastically about them. His own make-up was that of a simple, practi-cal man and so was that of most people. He would talk convincingly, persuasively to them on this topic. They did not need to do more, only do what they were doing, but with a right intention, with a divine pur-posefulness to it, offering their works for the intentions of the Sacred Heart, saying their beads and other prayers for the same intention. He worked out five intentions for the decades of the rosary, to remind them of this. Many parishes adopted those intentions for general use.

On some days he enrolled as many as three parishes, and before long practically all of the diocese of Muenster had joined the Apostleship of Prayer.

There was no sense of self-satisfaction in the splendid results of his efforts. His mind and heart seemed absorbed by a growing awareness of an immense field of additional labor. The work of the Apostleship led him to a realization of the apostolate of the foreign missions. Friends began to notice that he took occasion to express regrets, quite frequently, over the fact that Germany's interest in foreign mission work was negligible, and that, in comparison with other nations, it was far behind in its endeavors to train and send out missionaries. And this was not for him just a matter for small talk. He started to work energetically for the missionaries. He pleaded the cause of the foreign missions whenever he could and personally collected a considerable amount of donations, which he sent to missionaries in Africa.

And this interest and zeal was not a passing phase of his career. The work for the Apostleship, the interest in the apostolate of the missions grew steadily greater, absorbing all his thought. He had spent twelve years in teaching. Teaching was good, was apostolic. To form the minds and hearts of those who would later on be leaders of their fellow-men, that was important work. But there had been in him this growing desire to enter into a wider field, the direct field of influencing not a few but great numbers for the work and prayer that fulfilled Christ's desires. There was the much greater darkness of pagan nations that needed the light of the Word, and he felt that it was this work that God wanted of him.

61

He resolved to resign his professorship and devote himself entirely to the work of the Apostleship. It was a decision that meant giving up a permanent position and a career for which he had been specially trained and proven fit. He was now 36 years old. The financial outlook for the work he intended to devote himself to was extremely meager. If he were forced to seek another teaching position, later on, it would not be readily found. It was a serious step that he had in mind, and we can understand why his fellow priests did not approve of it. They told him it was a foolish notion, impractical, and that the Bishop would flatly refuse his consent.

Nothing daunted, Father Janssen went to Bishop Brinkman, the Bishop of Muenster, making the whole trip from Bocholt to Muenster on foot. He stopped at parishes as he went, combining the work for the Apostleship of Prayer with his journey. He came at last to Muenster. It was February, a cold month, but the Bishop gave him a cordially warm reception. He listened to the detailed explanation of Father Janssen and his desires: to do more for the spiritual welfare of the Church, especially for the foreign missions; to have leisure to edit a popular monthly magazine for promoting the spirit of prayer, and faith, and a wider working for the intentions of Christ. The Bishop immediately gave his approbation.

Without a moment's hesitation, Father Janssen proceeded to carry out his plans. He handed in his resignation as teacher at Bocholt, and left the school at the beginning of the summer vacation.

His immediate concern should have been to secure a domicile, a base of operations. Instead, he set out on a trip that was bound up with a new enterprise: the reunion of separated Christians in Germany. The noblest minds, both Catholic and non-Catholic, were deeply concerned with this great religious problem. For Father Janssen there was only one solution and it was a simple one: "The reunion of the Protestants with the Catholic Church is a work of divine grace; therefore, let us pray and make sacrifices in order to merit this grace and draw it down from Heaven." That was his solution of the matter — grace. And the sacrifice of the Mass was the most efficacious means of obtaining grace. So the first need was to have Masses said for this intention. He planned to have these Masses celebrated at the most important shrines in the country, especially at Fulda, the resting place of St. Boniface, the Apostle of Germany. He wanted, in particular, to gather sufficient funds to establish a perpetual fund for a daily Mass at Fulda. This Mass, to be said in honor of St. Boniface, who had laid the foundations of Christianity in Germany and had died a martyr to the work, would bring the grace that was needed. He had no doubt of that.

So he set out upon a journey through Germany and Austria to interest men prominent in public affairs. Bishop Brinkman's blessing he readily had. At Paderborn Bishop Conrad Martin encouraged him with a memorable sentence: "If we had prayed as much for protestant Germany as we have railed against it, it would have become catholic long ago."

His journey took him through Saxony and Bohemia to Silesia, thence to Vienna and Switzerland, with a return home by the way of southern Germany. It was a journey full of hardships and privations. He made a great part of the way on foot. In his frugality and severity, he often denied himself the most necessary things. One priest tells how he appeared at his door, "half frozen and famished." In Bohemia he was jailed by the police because of insufficient identification papers. In Switzerland he was held for three days in a hotel for the same reason. At times he was ridiculed and rudely sent away, even in places where he might rightfully have expected a kind reception. On the other hand he also won some unexpected friends.

The funds he collected were not sufficient to establish a perpetual fund for a daily Mass at Fulda. So he used it for having Masses said at various places of pilgrimage in Germany and Austria. Quietly, he kept on working at his idea, for many years, but the hoped for reunion never came to pass. The "May laws" only widened the breach between Catholics and Protestants, and all idea of reunion was eventually given up.

Chapter 8

FATHER JANSSEN'S attempt to assist in re-
uniting the Christians of Germany was a failure, but
strangely enough it was successful in another way. He
found a home. In the course of his travels he stopped
at a town called Kempen. There was a Convent of the
Ursulines here and they needed a chaplain. It was a
quiet place, and the duties of the chaplain would be
merely daily Mass and the giving of instructions in
Christian doctrine to the pupils of the Academy. He
would have ample time for other occupations, and, in
case of absence, a priest from the nearby city could be
secured for the daily Mass. With the consent of his
Bishop he accepted the position.

At once he began work on his contemplated religious magazine.

Despite his readiness as a youth to oblige his cousins
with a speech, and his ability to deliver it extempo-
raneously, Father Janssen had not developed into an

accomplished speaker. He had thoughts, coherence, zeal, piety, but not the charm of voice and presence that the great orators possess.

Once, when addressing a Catholic Convention, the only thing he seems to have succeeded in impressing his hearers with was the awkwardness of his delivery. A priest, who had something of a reputation as an orator, made a slighting remark about Father Janssen's presumption in putting himself at the head of an enterprise when "he can't even speak."

Others spoke more kindly of his effort, but the truth of the matter was that as far as public speaking was concerned he had the essentials, but lacked most of the accidentals.

He was aware of that, and perhaps thought of the printed word as a way to offset his personal defects as a speaker. Perhaps, too, he realized his projects and plans needed the widest possible audience. The printed word was far more permanent a thing than the spoken one, and it was definitely a power for wider good. Of that he was convinced.

In January, 1874, the first copy of his magazine, the *Little Messenger of the Sacred Heart,* appeared.

It comprised only eight pages, and was printed in Paderborn. All the work of wrapping and shipping was done by Father Janssen himself at Kempen. The makeup was very simple. There were articles of a purely devotional nature, and then there were narratives about home and foreign missions. In the devotional section, usually two pages, Father Janssen made frequent use of the writings of Anne Catherine Emmerick.

To promote the cause of the home missions, the *Little Messenger* frequently recommended the Society of St. Boniface, whose chief object was to aid the Catholics scattered through the Protestant sections of Germany.

The largest amount of space he gave over to articles about the foreign missions. He explained that as the chief object of his magazine: "The greatest and most meritorious of all works is the salvation of souls; it is the work of Christ Himself. He who aids in the propagation of the faith does not only save one soul, but many, the original convert and all his descendants.

"Take, for instance, the conversion of Germany to Christianity. How many holy men and women took part in this labor! It took years and the bearing of much suffering to accomplish this noble work. Hunger, thirst, cold, heat, weariness, danger, and disappointment were the stations the missionaries had to travel on the road to this great goal. We still enjoy the fruits of their labors. We are their children in the faith, and the glory of everlasting fatherhood rests on them in heaven. The work of the propagation of the faith is the first and noblest aim of God's Church on earth. To this sublime work our little magazine is dedicated."

The articles on the missions were thoroughgoing and interesting. They were filled with geographical and statistical information, they furnished data on natural science and the civilization and history of faraway countries. But entertainment and instruction were not the periodical's sole aim. It tried to arouse active interest in the mission cause.

Repeatedly, in calm, reasoned out sentences he showed his readers that the furthering of the mission spirit tends to make the gift of true faith more appreciated and loved at home. Interest in the missions deepened their own faith. The unhappiness of those in pagan darkness brings us a realization of the light of our own faith. The pains and labors of the missionaries to bring to the heathen the glad tidings of the gospel, can only fill us with new love for the faith which the good God gave us from youth.

The usual placidity of language and thought, which was almost second nature to him, could, however, suddenly disappear when urging aid for this great project. He wrote an article entitled: "China, the great land of the hopes and sorrows of Christ." In it he described the teeming masses of that vast country and tried to show how urgent was its need: "Every man has an immortal soul, even though he be a Mameluke or a negro. His body may be short or long, the color of his skin black or white, yellow or red — all these things are nonessential. He is and remains a human being possessed of a precious soul created after God's own image, made to know and love Him, and destined to be forever happy or unhappy.

"And all these millions of Chinese are pagans — that is, people for whom Christ as yet appears to have died in vain. They sin and there is no one to forgive their sins. They are in complete ignorance of God, of eternity, and of their rights and duties.

"What pains have been taken by the men of science to explore the interior of Africa and Australia! They have braved countless dangers; they have endured the scorching sun of tropical climes; they have forgone every comfort. And why? To enlarge our knowledge of these continents and also, possibly, to win a little renown for themselves.

"Others have penetrated the fields of eternal ice that surround the poles of our globe. They have buried themselves, as it were, in these cold regions, for weeks and months, camping under the open sky or living in tents. And to what purpose has all this been done? For the satisfaction of telling the world that they have come so many miles closer to the pole!

"What sacrifices are made for earthly fame and material gain! Oh, if but one half, nay one fourth, or even one tenth part of the efforts made for material ends were but spent for the greater intentions of Christ!

"May this great land of China, with its millions of heathens, become more and more, until the day of its salvation, a silent reproach to all Catholic nations."

This last remark referred mainly to Germany. It was a source of deep regret for him to have to see the disinterest his own country had for the foreign missions. He pointed out to them how far they lagged behind the missionary zeal of French Catholics. He exhorted them, he reasoned with them, he did everything in his power to rouse them. "Let us not say," he pleaded, "we have enough to do at home. The Lord says: 'Go ye to all nations.' These words may not be intended for each individual Christian but they are surely addressed to the great Catholic nations. We are all members of the Universal Church, and should at least be united in our desires and prayers."

But the country had trouble enough these days. It was too deeply immersed in the struggle for preserving its own faith to give heed to the need of other nations that had as yet no inkling of the faith. Father Janssen's little magazine was a voice crying in the wilderness, and all it had for its pains were empty echoes.

Chapter 9

$\mathcal{D}$URING the latter part of the nineteenth century, Germany was torn by political storm and strife. The Government, the Conservative Party, and especially the Liberals had united in an anti-Catholic movement to deprive the Church of its rights and self-government.

The Liberals were the instigators of this attack. They were opposed to all positive belief, and the cardinal point of their program was to secure for "free and independent science" absolute control over the intellectual life of the nation. They wanted to introduce that attitude into all departments of national life and education, even into the education of the clergy. That was their cultural philosophy (their Kultur) and the struggle (Kampf) for its achievement gave historians the name for this period of conflict — Kulturkampf.

The Liberals had always been exponents of national unity, and their platform of "free science" had been one of the means to that end. Bismarck had achieved national unity and they lined up at his side. As a Prussian official he belived in a State Church, a church that would not only be under the supervision of the State, but that would positively serve the purposes of the State.

With such a coalition drawn up against them the Catholics were hard-pressed to maintain any resemblance of religious liberty. As a final resort they were forced to band together into a political party of their own which was called the Center.

In May of 1873 an amendment was made to the constitution. The Catholic Church from now on, in all her administration, was to be subject to the laws of the State; and along with this amendment four bills were adopted that were aimed at making the Catholic Bishops independent of Rome, the clergy independent of the Bishops, and both of them dependent on the State. They were called the May laws from the fact of their being adopted in that historic month of May, 1873.

By means of these laws the education of the clergy was to depend upon the State and was to be carried out in the spirit of German liberalism. All ecclesiastical offices were to be filled only after approval by the civil authority. It became a criminal offense for any priest to exercise his priestly functions without authorization from the civil power.

Almost without exception the clergy followed the direction of their Bishops and repudiated these unjust laws. At once hundreds of them were fined for performing their priestly duties. None of the condemned priests would voluntarily pay these fines and so they were forcibly collected, to the great irritation and embitterment of the Catholic lay people. Then prison sentences were meted out. Seminarians were declared subject to military service. Church clubs and societies

71

6

were forbidden to exist, and the members of the Center were harassed and persecuted.

And, as the conflict grew, still other reprisals were exacted and heavier loads imposed on those whose sole fault was their loyalty to the faith of their fathers.

The core of the entire movement resided in the person of the Iron Chancellor, Bismarck. There was in him a fear of aggression from the East and there was in him a driving desire for world-wide supremacy. Both these moves he felt would be impossible of achievement without a national unity that would be complete and absolute.

It was in this period of political strife that Father Janssen moved, and he went about his work and activities with a calmness that had in it a touch of the hereditary. So many of his forbears had been born and lived through periods of even greater strife and war, and yet had emerged with their resplendent faith untouched.

It was a time when absolute freedom was demanded for scientific pursuits, a time of cold rationalism, of autocratic compulsion, of deification of the State. The trend of the times had their impact on Father Janssen. He loved science, but it was not a god for him, not a thing beyond all laws and restraint. It was not an absolute. It was just science, the seeking out of the laws hidden away in the things of creation, the formulating of those laws, so that earth and water, metal and matter could be used for the purposes of men. It could be a work of religion — seeking out the mind of the Creator in the marvelous laws He had implanted in creation. Science could be a guide showing the way to the greatness of the Author of Science.

The rationalism of his day left him cold. He was a very rational personality himself, but he had never been led astray by the pride of the intellect into its deification. Man is not only a thinking creature, he is a feeling creature, and his feelings also required fulfillment. To the rational love of science he joined the mystical delight of religious worship.

He was a child of his country, a German, but he was too a child of his Church, a Catholic. If his native land in its desire for world-wide achievements had turned the wrong way, and thought to achieve greater freedom by taking away the freedom of its own nationals, he did not make that error too. His Catholic heart had desires for world-wide achievements, not for his own self or glorification, but because such was the Will of the One whose way he had come to prepare. The true empire was the rule of the meek man of Nazareth, and it lay not in force or the glorification of the intellect, or the pride of nationalism, but in the depth of man's heart and its submission to Christ.

The Iron Chancellor had a view to world-wide conquest — for his nation and his personal renown. And the quiet priest had too, a vision of world-wide conquest but it was for the Kingdom of God and for the fulfillment of the desires of the Sacred Heart. He himself did not enter into the picture, except as the one who would pray for that, and, by means of an insignificant little magazine, ask other people to pray, and point out to them how they could work for that glorious world-cause.

Because of the "May laws" many priests had been exiled from Germany and were adrift in the adjacent countries. Father Janssen had met some of them, he had heard of others who eked out an existence while waiting for the persecution to abate so that they could return to their native land and the work that had been taken from their hands. He thought often of these shepherds without a flock. He prayed for them, and it came to him that there was a definite place and task awaiting them.

In the June number of his magazine he addressed an appeal to these priests and also to seminarians who were about to be ordained. "Is there no one throughout our wide country," he asked, "who feels the call to devote himself to the cause of the missions? Would it not be possible for German priests to band together and found a German Mission Seminary in some safe region outside the homeland? That would be a project in complete accord with the wishes of the Propaganda in Rome, and with the express desire of the Holy Father himself.

"Belgium, Ireland, Italy, France — all have their mission seminaries. Italy has four of them; and the city of Paris alone, five. And Germany, where there are so many truly Christian families, has, thus far, not even one.

"We feel that this state of affairs should continue no longer; and if there are any in sympathy with the idea voiced above and willing to unite to this end, we gladly offer our services to bring the project about, in so far as we are able."

Father Janssen was 37 years old when he penned that appeal. For those who knew him, the idea he proposed must have been a great surprise. It had been so plainly apparent from all his previous enterprises that his interests lay completely in things spiritual: Masses for the

74

intentions of the Sacred Heart, the Apostleship of Prayer, Masses for the reunion of Protestant Germany. Now, suddenly, he blossoms forth with the idea of building a seminary for training priests for the foreign missions.

The project was completely out of character. He was quiet, unpretentious, and profoundly simple. His simplicity, his singleness of mind, had always been his outstanding characteristic. Up to the present he had had only one interest — exclusively spiritual matters.

It was not a pose. They knew that. But this sudden shift of ground into agitating for the founding of a seminary, into trying to organize exiled priests for foreign missionary work, this seemed to give the lie to the man's simplicity. He was not simple, he was complex. He had aspirations along other lines than the ones they had imagined to be his exclusive pursuit.

As yet none of them had come to the truth about Father Janssen. There was force, latent intensity, banked up enthusiasm behind that silent exterior. These qualities seldom showed, except when some enterprise beckoned which appeared to be the Will of God. His first enterprises had been activities of a completely spiritual nature. To his friends they were projects peculiarly fitting for Father Janssen's make-up — small and pious. They failed to see that he had taken up these projects, not because his simplicity was the kind that was absorbed in small things and pietistic things, but because his simplicity was of the kind that has a single, dominant purpose — the Will of God. All his initial enterprises, at the time of their doing, had seemed to be God's Will for him. Devotedly, wholeheartedly, he had spent on them time, thought, work and prayer.

And the net result, excepting his work for the Apostleship of Prayer, had been failure.

These failures seemed not to have greatly disturbed him. Possibly, they only made him wonder if he had not rushed into tasks that others might have brought to a more successful issue. But his eagerness for the interests of God, his childlike faith did not alter. He knew that his intention had been right, that he had not been concerned with selfish aims but with God's Will, and that the prayer he had brought to each enterprise had not been wasted. Prayer never is. But the setbacks encountered in these projects would have normally slowed down a man, and would have made him somewhat cautious about attempting anything new. Instead Father Janssen comes forth with a much wider, more vitally opportune, and yet more difficult undertaking.

A vague suspicion may have crossed the minds of his acquaintances that this quiet priest's stolidity was a mask covering an internal restlessness, that his placidity was a disguise for a spirit which craved the limelight. He had never shown any desire for a place of prominence, but that may have been because he had been biding his time. There seemed to be no other explanation for this unexpected reversal of form in the man they knew, except possibly that he had been overwhelmed by some pietistic brainstorm. But that was an explanation that did not make sense, for he was too steady-going, too deliberate in all that he did and said.

That deliberatenesss was the key to what was to them a mystery. When Father Janssen voiced an idea it was never an idea that he had just recently come by. He moved slowly, always, because he wanted his basis of action to be not just his own view of the matter, but

God's. "All with God." That was the way his father had taken up his daily work, or had faced any of the decisions in the simple life of a farmer and a teamster. That, too, was the son's way. And what God's desires were, a man did not, as a rule, discover overnight. Assurance about them came from prayer, much prayer, from the prayerful consideration of events, from the careful studying of needs, from humble attention to the Church's guidance.

In 1866, the Missionary Society of the Holy Ghost, founded in France by Father Paul Libermann, opened a German Mission Seminary in the old abbey of Marienstatt in Germany. They had eight clerical students, and twenty novices for the brotherhood. The War of 1870 hampered the development of the institution, and the Kulturkampf closed it in 1872.

This event took place while Father Janssen was a professor at Bocholt. It was at that very period of his life when his work for the Apostleship of Prayer was leading him into an awareness of the tremendous scope and need of the foreign missions.

The opening of that first German Mission Seminary was a profound joy for him; its closing, a bitter regret and sudden disillusion. But it was not merely that. He, who had known failures enough himself, found in this failure of another man a spur and a challenge that stirred him as no other single event ever had.

With his usual reserve he said nothing to anyone about the impact this event had upon him. An idea had been kindled, like a vital spark within his soul, but he kept it quietly to himself. For a year he held it in his heart. Under the influence of grace and prayer the idea that had come to him germinated slowly, steadily, surely, into a solid and established conviction.

77

The following year, when he decided to give up his position at Bocholt his family were considerably upset. They wrote expressing their misgivings at his leaving such a fine position. In reply he told them that a nobler and worthier cause had laid its claim on him, and stated that he intended to work for the founding of a German Mission Seminary.

His family knew of his intentions, but no one else. It was his way not to mention his plans to others, waiting always for a propitious moment to make them public. Such an occasion presented itself in May of 1874.

The Prefect Apostolic of Hong Kong, Bishop Raimondi, was visiting Germany as the guest of Father Ludwig von Essen, the pastor of Neuwerk. Father Janssen had heard of the Bishop's arrival and decided to visit him in order to obtain information and material about the foreign missions for his magazine.

The Bishop received Father Janssen very kindly. He poured out an abundance of information about the missions in China. Bishop Raimondi was everything that Father Janssen had expected him to be. A man of experience, a successful and courageous missionary, a man whose whole soul was alive with zeal for the great cause he was serving. His dynamic recital about the missions in China deeply impressed him. His eyes glowed as he heard of the glorious work that was being done by priests and Brothers and Sisters in those far-off fields so white for the harvest. These were the things his father had read to him as a boy, and they were real, and still being carried on. His eyes grew wistful. "Would I be too old now to be a missionary?" he asked hesitantly.

78

Bishop Raimondi looked up at him. "That is not necessary," he replied. Father Janssen's face fell. "I mean, for you to go in person to the missions. Priests are needed very much at home to work for the cause of the foreign missions."

At great length he detailed the work he had done as a co-founder of two mission seminaries — the Milan Seminary for Foreign Missions, the Mission House of Mill Hill in England.

Father Janssen listened attentively and when the Bishop had finished he told him of his attempts to interest, through his magazine, some priests in founding a mission seminary. None had replied. Shamefacedly, he admitted to the Bishop that he had not been able to interest anyone in undertaking so vital a project.

Bishop Raimondi studied the apparently deep and real sorrow that clouded his visitor's face. "Well, then, why don't you do it yourself?" Startled, Father Janssen's eyes jumped up to meet the Bishop's gaze. "I mean it. Found one yourself."

Thorough amazement and disbelief showed in Father Janssen's candid eyes. Calmly, intently, the Bishop met his gaze. He liked what he saw. The amazement and fright were genuine, and it would be only a true and deep humility that would underlay them. "What are you looking so frightened for?" he asked. "If the work is to be started, some one must start it."

"Yes, of course," agreed Father Janssen slowly, "but I am not capable of starting such a work." He looked down at his hands folded in his lap. "The thought of doing it myself never entered my mind."

"Well, then, join up with Father von Essen and work together for that purpose."

"Father von Essen?"

"Yes. He has already done some of the preliminary work." He told him then that Father von Essen had submitted a plan to both the Archbishop of Cologne and to the Propaganda in Rome for founding a German Mission Seminary. The replies had been the same. Both the Archbishop and Rome doubted the advisability of starting such a work under the difficult political conditions then existing in Germany, but they gave it their approbation and blessing.

It was indeed a welcome surprise for Father Janssen to learn that another priest had already been working so actively and successfully for the idea which he had been cherishing in silence and prayer. But Bishop Raimondi's suggestion that he now align himself with Father von Essen left him cold. He would not consider it. He was willing to help, by prayer and by means of his little magazine, but to be a founder or co-founder of such a great enterprise was something he had neither dreamed of nor desired.

But Bishop Raimondi would not be put off. The more he talked with this plain priest, the more he seemed to see in him something eminently fitted for this great cause. He multiplied reasons and arguments, he employed every persuasion. To no avail. And yet the Bishop would not admit defeat. "I shall call on you in Kempen," he finally said, terminating the interview, "and I shall urge this matter upon you even more strongly."

He did come to Kempen, twice, but all his exhortations that Father Janssen should take this important task upon himself were in vain. The only thing he was able to wrest from him was the promise that he would work for this great cause to the best of his ability, that he would bring it to the attention of the public through his *Little Messenger*, that he would try to arouse interest in it. He had not changed Father Janssen's mind in the least, for that had been Father Janssen's original idea of how he would assist and share in this great work.

In the next number of his magazine he published an appeal, addressed to priests and seminarians, for starting a mission seminary. There was no response. That did not discourage him. It was only meant as the opening shot in what would be a persistently waged campaign. The conduct of that campaign concerned him. He wanted it to be handled so practically and energetically that Catholic Germany would be thoroughly stirred up. For that reason he paid a visit to Father von Essen and discussed with him ways and means to achieve that result.

Father von Essen had a presence. Everything about him spoke of culture and refinement. His mental abilities were of a very high order. He was a linguist of rare ability, speaking and writing fluently German, Italian and French. By all human standards, he was eminently fitted to head this new enterprise, for besides his gifts of birth and ability, he was a capable priest, and alive with true missionary zeal.

He was everything that Father Janssen was not, but they had one thing in common — their love for the cause of the foreign missions. They exchanged views about the projected mission seminary and the means to arouse interest in it. At the end of the deliberations Father von Essen brought up the matter of Father Janssen's formally aligning himself with him in this work, as Bishop Raimondi had suggested. The frank quiet eyes of Father Janssen met his for a moment, then he shook his head in refusal. Father von Essen pressed him for a reason, and the reply was frankly, quietly given. He did not think their characters would harmonize. There was no reproach meant. It was that practical, realistic attitude that was second nature to Father Janssen. A team of horses had to be compatible or no work would be done, only damage. He and Father von Essen were not compatible.

It took courage to tell a man of Father von Essen's standing such a truth, and it marred the friendliness of their meeting. But it was not allowed to destroy what they had come together for.

The results of their lengthy discussions were condensed by Father von Essen into an article for publication. In it he pointed out the great need and the opportunities for foreign mission work. He brought forward the example of other nations, and exhorted the clergy of Germany not to be outdone in their Catholicity. He proposed the founding of a foreign mission seminary as the first and essential step, and urged priests and seminarians to join this great cause. From the lay folk he asked the material aid that would make the plan a reality.

The article was well-written, by a man of considerable name, it was run in all the Catholic publications, and it had not a single response. Like a nice shiny pebble it had been dropped into the huge pool of the nation's life, and it slipped to the bottom, unnoticed, with only the faintest of ripples to show where the waters had closed over it.

Father Janssen too had published the article, in his *Little Messenger,* and along with it had urgently asked his readers to pray for this great project. To his mind, prayer was the essential need for the entire enterprise and during this decisive period he prayed unceasingly.

In the fields outside of the town of Kempen there had been erected the Stations of the Cross. It became a familiar sight, during these days, for the townsfolk to see the chaplain of the Ursuline Convent, hat in hand, slowly, reverently, praying his way from station to station. He used to do that daily, but now he took so much more time, and seemed so much more intent that they wondered what great need could have come upon the simple, good man.

One of the houses adjoining the convent was flanked by a small garden. The owner was wont to do his gardening at eventide. The window of Father Janssen's room was directly opposite, and many an evening the preoccupied priest forgot to draw his blinds. His neighbor, straightening up from his gardening, had a clear view of the lamp lit room and all it contained. More than once he would call his children out into the garden: "Come along, young ones, I want to show you something." They would follow him out into the garden and gather about him. He gestured toward the window. "See? That's how a saint prays." Awed, the children stared at Father Janssen, kneeling like a statue in his room, motionless and absorbed in God. The children would go scampering back to their play, but at odd moments they would steal back into the garden to peer again through the window. And always the priest knelt in the same place, his head bowed in prayer.

Days and weeks dragged by, and despite all Father

Janssen's prayer not the faintest ripple of interest appeared. Nobody seemed to care anything about starting a mission seminary. And yet the glory of God, the salvation of souls, the good of the Church, the example of other nations, and the spiritual advantage for the sorely tried Catholics of Germany seemed proof abundant that now was the time to begin a mission seminary.

It was true that the persecution of the Church in Germany would necessitate building the mission seminary outside of Germany. That was a drawback. It would be in a foreign country, not on German soil. But still there were so many candidates for the priesthood who could not, because of anti-Catholic laws, complete their studies, that there should have been an abundance of applicants interested in the possibility of finishing their training. At least, there should have been no lack of priests, deprived of pastoral work, who would have volunteered to act as teachers in this seminary. And yet not a single one had replied.

Father Janssen began to think that, perhaps, the reason for this complete disregard was that no one had been mentioned, by name, to whom application could be made. It grew apparent to his practical mind, that their efforts to arouse interest were too much along the lines of talk and not deeds. The whole project was hanging in the air. A place had to be chosen, a building put up, a seminary opened. What the whole idea needed was a sense of reality, an existing reality, not a hoped for one.

Father von Essen he knew would not be able to act directly as the head of the undertaking. The anti-Catholic regulations of the Government made that impossible. If he left his parish it would remain without a priest, for the "May laws" would not allow a new pastor to be appointed. Because of that the Archbishop could not permit Father von Essen to be relieved of his pastorate.

Minutely, very carefully, Father Janssen thought over the matter. Next to Father von Essen it seemed that he himself was the only one interested in the work. There was no reason why he could not give up his present position and undertake the project, if he chose. Up to the present moment he had not had any idea along those lines. He had declined all requests and invitations toward heading the work. And now he began to ask himself whether circumstances did not demand a different attitude? He asked himself seriously whether it was the Will of God that he should keep himself in a minor role, free from responsibility, safe from criticisms?

He looked back over his life and there were a number of events that could be construed as a divinely arranged training and preparation for just such a work as he now contemplated. There were his twelve years of experience as a teacher; his experience in the Apostleship of Prayer; his meetings with the hierarchy in the cause of the home missions; his growing interest and zeal for the foreign missions. There was, too, that blunt invitation, that had sounded almost like a command coming from the mouth of the Bishop: "Found one yourself."

He could recall the time he had gone to Father Perger with his carefully thought out and greatly cherished theory of numbers. The advice of Father Perger had caused him to drop the whole project, for there could very well have been a subtle pride underlying the whole enterprise.

85

There could be a hidden pride here, too, except that this project was not a personal theory but a divine reality. This was directly concerned with the command of Christ to "go into the whole world and teach the gospel to all people.' And he had enough experience already with various undertakings to know that there were far more rebuffs and heartaches and toil connected with any new project than personal glory. He had no thoughts of self. He had no desire to be at the head of anything. He had been sincere when he said that, and in his own heart he knew that that attitude of his had not changed. But events seemed compelling him to assume the role of leader, or else let the whole project die away into forgetfulness. It was a job that had to be done, and while several had spoken of it, no one seemed ready or able to assume the onus of putting his name to the project and assuming all the cares and responsibilities for its success or failure.

These considerations grew gradually, under the influence of much prayer, into firm convictions. In the autumn of 1874 he decided to attempt the founding of a mission seminary.

With that decision a phase of his life came to an end, and looking back over the years, there came to him the realization that what had brought him to this crossroads of decision had been his childlike conviction, his unquestioning faith in the all-importance of prayer. Memories crowded up in him of the days at home, the prayers he had listened to and shared in. This had been the foundation of it all. For from his earliest youth he had grasped the importance of prayer, not merely as some instrument to be used in time of need, but as an actual mode of life. It was a living communication between the Creator and the creature. One of the things that had drawn him to the priesthood had been that by it he obtained the power to offer up the supreme prayer of praise, of thanksgiving, of impetration and of atonement. In the priesthood he had seen the possibility not only of living this prayer life completely but of imparting it to others.

So he had tried to enlist priests in a group that would offer Mass each Friday for the intentions of the Sacred Heart; he strove for the reunion of Christians through prayer and Masses; his Apostleship of Prayer work was bound up intimately with prayer, and each edition of his *Little Messenger of the Sacred Heart* opened with a prayer and closed with one. One thing he seemed always to have been sure of. Prayer was the mightiest of means. Prayer was his life. An abundant life. With it all things were possible, even the realization of those vast desires that the Heart of God held. And prayer was possible to all, yet so few used it. He had wanted to arouse men to that fact, he had wanted to unite them in prayer, a concerted prayer that would infallibly persuade the gracious God to bring about the desires of His own Heart, to overcome the darkness and indifference of men and unite all of them in the one fold, and the true faith.

With genuine humbleness he had not visioned where such a desire might lead him. He had wanted only to give to others this great good, this deep awareness of the treasure he had. And most of his efforts had been barren of success. He admitted that. But all these successive failures now seemed to have had a purpose. By them there had come a gradual clearing up of his aims, a gentle guidance toward a work which he loved,

7

but which was out of all proportion to his abilities or desires. Yet that was of no consequence. His own desires never would be, nor his abilities. Only one thing mattered: what God wanted, how he wanted it, and who He wanted to do it. And it seemed that He wanted a mission seminary, and that he was to make the start for founding it.

By slow degrees he had come to a realization of how the things he had prayed for could be realized in this new work. In the founding of the seminary for training foreign missionaries he would unite a group of young men, who would not only bring about Christ's Kingdom on earth by going to the nations yet in darkness, but who would also carry on all the other good works of growth in faith and deepening of faith that he had visioned as the desires of Christ's heart. They would be men of science and men of prayer.

And at this moment only a profound sense of joy and gratefulness filled him. He could see that here in one stroke all his projects and plans for the glory of God could be fulfilled. Anything done for God was worth while, but this was supremely important. A training school for apostles. This would be his life.

Chapter 10

FATHER JANSSEN might be ultra-cautious in approaching a decision, but once it was made he moved into definite action. He knew that the site for a mission seminary would have to be as near the German border as possible, since it would have to draw most if its teachers, students and support from Germany, and so would need easy access to the homeland.

He went to the little Dutch border town of Venlo and enlisted the aid of a priest by the name of Father Moubis. Father Moubis promised to seek out a suitable estate for the mission seminary.

Father Janssen returned to Kempen. The following week a man appeared at his door. He had been sent by Father Moubis to offer him his estate at Tegelen. The next day, the 29th of September, was the Feast of St. Michael. At his Mass Father Janssen asked for the aid and guidance of the archangelic leader of the heavenly hosts, promising to name the seminary in his honor.

After Mass he went to Mr. Ludwig Boenner, a farmer from Kempen, and asked him to make the trip with him and help him in appraising the property. The man readily consented, and together they journeyed across the border to Tegelen.

The property seemed in every way suitable for a seminary, but when the owner named his price Mr. Boenner's indignation knew no bounds. Seventy five thousand marks was an outrageous price. He advised Father Janssen to make no offer at all. The negotiations came to an abrupt end.

They returned to Kempen. But Father Janssen could not get the picture of the Tegelen estate out of his mind. It was a beautiful location, ideal for his purpose. He decided, after some time, to visit the owner in person and make further efforts to obtain it. He made two trips for this purpose. On the first one he reopened the negotiations for the property. On the second one he proved that if he was no orator, yet the art of persuasive speech was not entirely unknown to him. He managed to have the price brought down to 45,000 marks; thirty thousand marks lower than the original price asked. A contract was drawn up for that amount granting him a six weeks' option.

The property was located in the diocese of Roermond, and so Father Janssen visited the ordinary, Bishop Paeredis, and obtained permission to open the contemplated seminary in his diocese. It was a great day for Father Janssen. He came away from the Bishop's residence starry-eyed with the success of these first steps. The location had been found, and the local Bishop's permission granted. His simplicity and zeal seemed to have left him totally unaware of the kind of reaction his project might have on others.

Inside the episcopal residence, one of the local pastors had just entered Bishop Paeredis' office. The Bishop was a busy man and the pastor was ready to present his request in as few words as possible. But the Bishop gave him no opening. He seemed rather distracted and kept tapping the heel of a pencil idly against the top of his desk. "I had a visitor just now," he finally said. "A Father Janssen."

"Father Janssen?" echoed the pastor politely. "From the diocese, your excellency?"

"No. He's from Kempen. Chaplain of an Ursuline convent there. He wants to build at Tegelen ... a mission seminary — and he has no funds."

The priest made a commiserating sound, but the Bishop did not even look at him. He was too preoccupied with the memory of Father Janssen's face and figure. The eyes, so alert, so warm, so filled with the lights of an enthusiast, a visionary — and then that sturdy line of jaw, and a chin like granite. What a curious, curious person! "He is either a fool," he said slowly, "or a saint."

The pastor stared at the Bishop. He had merely come to see him about a dispensation from a matrimonial impediment, and he was being treated to somebody's biography, somebody who was either a fool or a saint. If the man was going to build a seminary without money he could tell the Bishop exactly what the man was.

Abruptly the Bishop put the pencil down, hitched his chair forward. He was the executive again. "Yes, Father?" he asked crisply. The pastor came forward, hurriedly drawing some documents from his coat pocket. For the time being Father Janssen's personal status was forgotten.

The disclosures which the Bishop had made about Father Janssen's project were true, but they were not complete.

Father Janssen had no money to build a seminary. There were also other things which he did not have. He had no students to put in the seminary, and he had no professors to teach them. In fact he had absolutely nothing but an option on a piece of property, and six weeks in which to get the money to pay for it.

At once he went to work to raise the amount needed. He published an appeal in his magazine, entreating his readers to help him. A few meager offerings were sent in.

Nothing daunted, Father Janssen started out on a journey to obtain both men and money. He went to the seminaries at Roermond, of Luxemburg, and the American College at Louvain, trying to interest some students of theology to join him in his work. Everywhere he was given a kind reception, everywhere his aspirations were commended, but nowhere did he get a single student. Nor did he get any financial support.

Disheartened by the complete failure of his trip, and suffering from a serious chest condition, he came back from his journey. There was work aplenty awaiting him. The first annual report on his *Little Messenger of the Sacred Heart,* which now had 3,000 subscribers, demanded his immediate attention. He was ill and exhausted from his trip and the talks which had been completely fruitless. He had to raise the money to purchase the property at Tegelen. Where was he to raise that amount? How was he to arouse the interest of seminarians and priests? If he did not raise the money soon all his preliminary work would go for naught. If he did not have students and professors to staff it, he would have an empty house. Sick and disappointed he was sorely tempted to drop the entire idea. "Why work so hard?" he asked himself. "Nothing will come of it anyway.... It's the same kind of treatment that others got who tried to start this work. It would not be quite so bad if I had good health, but I am sick and exhausted almost to the point of death, and yet I will have to labor like a healthy man. It is a pretty gloomy outlook. And this is only the beginning...!"

Chapter 11

 HERE WAS too much childlike trust in Father
Janssen's heart for him to remain long a prey to heavy
thoughts. The complete failure of his initial efforts and
the discouraging fact of his ill health were trials that,
after the first dark moments, he manfully shouldered.
But out of that experience came the realization that he
could not go ahead without the general public's knowledge and support of him and his cause. It was his firm
belief that the enterprise was God's design, and he was
sure that his confidence in God would carry him
through all future trials and troubles. But his personal
faith alone was not enough to inspire others with confidence in this undertaking. He realized that he was
expecting too much if he imagined that students of
theology would abandon their carreers and join a man
who could give them no assurance as to their future.
And it was asking a great deal to expect people to
advance large sums of money for the promotion of a

94

cause, which, under the prevailing conditions, seemed hardly likely to succeed. The whole project needed the open support of those in authority and it needed publicity.

He made up his mind to visit the hierarchy of Germany, Austria and Holland, tell them about his plans, and ask for their blessings and recommendation. There was, too, the hope that funds might be gathered in time to save the situation. The six weeks were not yet up.

In January of 1875 he set out on another trip. His first visit was to his own Bishop, Bishop J. Brinkmann of Muenster. When the Bishop heard of the sum which Father Janssen was supposed to raise in a few weeks, he shook his head in doubt. However, he gave him a cautiously worded letter of approbation.

The following morning Father Janssen said Mass at a Franciscan monastery. One of the Fathers had learned of Father Janssen's pressing need for financial assistance, and urged him to speak about the matter with their Provincial, Father Gregory. He was in the monastery just then on a visitation.

A religious congregation has, as a rule, financial problems of its own, but the good Franciscan was so insistent, and so confident that his provincial would help, that Father Janssen acceded.

An interview was arranged for him, and, in the presence of the Superior of the monastery, he poured out for Father Gregory the tale of his plans and needs and failures. When he had finished, Father Gregory leaned back. "Forty five thousand marks? That can be arranged. See Bishop Haneberg of Speyer. He is a great friend of the missions. Ask him for a recommendation, and then apply to the Ludwigsverein in Munich; they will give you the money." Then turning to the Superior of the monastery, he asked him: "Do you not know of some person interested in the missions to whom you might recommend Father Janssen? Let both of us do something for this great cause; it will no doubt make our last hour easier for us."

This ready interest and evident willingness to help greatly encouraged Father Janssen. He plodded faithfully off to the people recommended and laid his financial needs before them. All his efforts were in vain. He did not receive the money.

The six weeks were up and he had to cancel the contract. Regretfully he faced the fact that he must aim at a smaller and a much less expensive beginning.

The one bright spot in this setback was his meeting with Father Gregory. The fact that a man of such vision and experience had readily approved, and so wholeheartedly tried to assist the undertaking, did him a world of good.

He went on to meet the Archbishop of Cologne. This venerable prelate, Archbishop Melchers, in championing the cause of religious freedom had experienced, in his own person, the harsh vindictiveness of the Government's iron hand. From the 31st of March to the 9th of September, 1874, he had been in prison. He faced now the prospect of new conflicts with the Government, a host of perplexing problems and personal sufferings. Father Janssen found the prelate in a rather depressed state of mind. He knew of the trials that the Archbishop had gone through, and the new ones he now faced, and so he laid the plans for his project before him as succinctly as possible. When he had finished, the Archbishop stared at him in astonishment and said, "We are living in a time when everything is tottering and threatening to collapse; and now you come and wish to build up something new?"

Father Janssen replied: "Forgive me, Your Grace, for bringing up such a project at a time like this. It is true we live in a time when many things are going to ruin; and so, new things must rise in their place. The very fact that newly ordained priests are not allowed to work in their own country, should turn their eyes toward the foreign missions."

The deep sincerity of his visitor impressed the prelate. But he was too burdened with the critical state of affairs between the Church and the Government to have much time for anything else. He remembered that this project had originally been broached by one of his own priests, Father von Essen, and he recommended Father Janssen to take up the matter with him. The two of them were to draw up a memorandum in writing about the whole matter, so that he could see how much of a start had actually been made and what prospects of success the venture might hold.

When Father Janssen left the room the harassed Archbishop turned to his secretary. "Can you imagine that? Found a seminary and train missionary priests for the conversion of the pagans! In these critical times! There are pagans enough in Cologne; if he would only convert them first!"

There was no encouragement whatsoever from his visit with the two Bishops, and word began to filter around in clerical circles about Father Janssen and his rather wild-eyed plans. His friends and acquaintances in the priesthood urged him to drop the whole idea. They told him it was excessive piety, stupidity. Even his former teacher, Father Perger, when he heard of Father Janssen's ambitious ideas, was stirred to vocal protest. He plainly declared that Father Janssen should not go about making a fool of himself, that such an enterprise at a time like this was absolutely impossible, moreover, he stated bluntly, Father Janssen was not the right man to carry out such a work. And that opinion was almost unanimously echoed by all the priests who knew him: he did not have the necessary qualities for founding a mission seminary.

Their concerted judgment must have seriously shaken Father Janssen's confidence. Humbly he went to a good friend of his, Father Fugemann of Kempen, and asked him what he would advise him to do. The priest replied: "Go ahead! You are just the man for this kind of thing. You have all the qualities needed: stubbornness, piety, a sufficiently impractical mind."

It was said half-jokingly, half-seriously, and it was not exactly the kind of answer Father Janssen had expected. He was hesitating, doubtful, confused. He had wanted a long, serious talk, a discussion of his perplexing problem. It was possible, by thought and prayer, to come to a fairly clear judgment as to what God's Will was on a certain matter. But when all the people who knew you best assured you that you were not the one to be handling the project, it made a man doubt whether they were not right. After all, there was in every man a pride that could deceive him into attempting what God did not want him to attempt. And this enterprise of a mission seminary was too important for his inadequacy to ruin it. From the outset he had been deeply aware of his lack of those personal qualities which his colleagues now were pointing out to him. It had kept him from starting the project until circumstances had so fallen out that it seemed that God wanted him to head it. Bishop Raimondi's words; all his thoughts and prayers about the matter; the impossibility of Father von Essen to start it; and the total lack of interest because no one would put his name to the project. All these things had all pointed one way. So he had gone ahead, and now everyone told him to stop.

In his trouble he had turned to one who knew him and who would give him a true evaluation, a blunt answer. The evaluation had been blunt enough, but it had held also a smile. As though he were tilting with windmills. He was stubborn and impractical — and pious. He was a priest; a priest was supposed to be pious. It was something taken for granted. Father Fugemann had meant more than that; he had been alluding to all his previous attempts that involved purely religious undertakings. His friend had meant that he was so obsessed with the devotional aspect of things that he saw only the spiritual side of the seminary project and forgot that it entailed a very practical aspect: money, men, property, buildings, administration. And he was "sufficiently impractical." He knew that, and had admitted it to himself and to God, many times, in the secrecy of his soul. But it was not because he did not see what was to be done and how to do it, it was because a man must know how to doubt and question prudently in order to find out God's Will. And he was stubborn. He would not give up. He had to have answers. But they did not understand. He didn't want the answer to this problem for his own sake, to be able to say proudly to the world, "There, see, I've solved the difficulty. Germany has a mission seminary and great numbers of priests have found work for their hands." That meant nothing. What only meant anything to him was that the desire of Christ's heart be fulfilled, that the Will of God be accomplished. And this had seemed by all the ordinary ways of judgment to be what He desired. And yet all those who were qualified to know assured him that he was pushing himself into a work for which he was totally unfitted. Who was he to doubt their concerted opinion? They were priests, teachers, experienced pastors, sure in their worldly knowledge and judgments.

It was a dark period, and in it he took to prayer and walked the way of the cross daily, waiting.

He prayed much to St. Joseph. The pious Bishop Adams of Luxemburg had told him to recommend his financial needs to him, and suddenly, during the month of March, a ray of light pierced the gloom. A Convent of Poor Clares had received a sizeable sum of money as a gift, but they wished to turn it over to some other good work. The Superioress had read about the contemplated mission seminary in the *Little Messenger* and thought of donating the money to that cause. She conferred with a priest about the matter and he decided to have a personal interview with Father Janssen.

After a lengthy conference the two priests formulated a message which was sent by wire to the nuns: "The founding of a mission seminary is a matter of great importance. If it now fails to succeed, no one, for a long time to come, will make a new attempt. Decide the matter for yourselves. Hold a novena, and if necessary, a second one. If you feel impelled to donate the money for this cause, do so; if not, retain it."

The longer the nuns prayed, the more they felt inclined to give the money for the mission seminary. Eventually they came to a decision and sent the money to Father Janssen.

The arrival of that donation stirred Father Janssen deeply. As such it meant nothing to him. He had never been of the acquisitive type. His own prize money he had spent in one grand gesture on his father. He was fully aware that money possessed the power to do good; but this particular gift had greater significance for him than just that.

He had been waiting, praying and waiting, for the Divine Will to manifest itself. If it were His design that Arnold Janssen should head this enterprise, then He would have to arrange matters, for he was unable of himself to decide his own fitness or unfitness, and, his own resources seemed at an end.

The wording of the telegram shows that he made no attempt to persuade or pressure the nuns. Their reaction to the message would be to him, in great measure, an indication of God's Will.

With great joy and thankfulness he received their decision and donation. Their mind had been made up for them in prayer. He looked at the check and knew that this was the right kind of money to put to work for God. It came from devoted hearts, self-sacrificing ones, the poor. It would beget riches, real riches for souls.

And as though to confirm matters for him beyond all doubt another gift arrived. A servant girl, Katherine Schell, donated six thousand marks for the seminary. She had inherited this sum from her wealthy employers

101

and wished to devote it to some pious work. She asked the advice of a Franciscan Father, and he referred the matter to his Provincial, Father Gregory. Father Gregory promptly advised that the money be given to Father Janssen for the new mission seminary.

This generous attitude of Father Gregory deeply touched Father Janssen, for he was well aware that the banishment of all religious from Germany was imminent, and Father Gregory could have found very good use for that money in establishing a new home for the Franciscan Fathers who would be sent into exile.

Hard upon the heels of these two windfalls there came a belated result from his trip to the seminaries. A student at the American College at Louvain, Francis Reichart, decided to join Father Janssen. Another letter from a pastor in Luxemburg, Father Peter Bill, informed him of his willingness to join, and that he had already received permission from his Bishop. *The Little Messenger of the Sacred Heart* had found its way into the Seminary of Ratisbon, in Bavaria, and one of the students John Baptist Anzer, who had already received minor orders, applied for admission and was readily accepted.

With breath-taking suddenness Father Janssen found himself possessed of a goodly sum of money and three co-workers. All his doubts and indecision were swept away. He was sure now, confident, that this was the work God wanted him to do.

He had some conferences with Father von Essen as Archbishop Melchers had directed, and together they drew up a report of the progress, the aims and means of their projected mission seminary. Since Father von Essen could not leave his parish and go to Holland,

102

Father Janssen was to have a free hand in the internal direction of the seminary, and in important external matters he would consult with Father von Essen. The foundation was to be considered as a common work of the two.

The report to the Archbishop was written by Father Janssen, in the rectory of Father von Essen, and was signed by both priests. The somewhat lengthy report caused the Archbishop to view the contemplated foundation more favorably. He sent his approbation, good wishes, and blessing.

Father Janssen expected men and means, not only from Germany but also from Austria and Holland, and for that reason it seemed the wise thing to inform the hierarchy of all these three countries about their undertakings.

First he visited the Bishops of Holland. All gave their approbation. Then he journeyed through Western and Southern Germany, to Brixon and Salzburg and back home through Austria and Bohemia. All the Bishops of Germany and Austria whom he visited gave him a kind reception and approved of his work. In all, twenty-eight German, Austrian and Dutch Bishops expressed themselves favorably in regard to the founding of the mission seminary and gave it their approbation and blessing.

Although this journey did not bring in a large amount of material support, he came home with high hopes, ready and eager to go ahead with his work.

There had been disappointments enough, there had been doubt and darkness, but the eventual success and the ensuing light more than made up for everything. He would remember much from these hard days of traveling and pleading, of rebuffs and disinterest, of prayer, patience and abandonment, but out of it all one thing would remain undyingly clear in his memory — the turning point had come from the hand of the poor. What the future would bring he did not know, whether the work would prosper or just dwindle back into nothingness, but one thing he did know and would never forget — that his work would owe its start to the generosity and sacrifices of the poor.

Chapter 12

A NEW DAY had dawned for Father Janssen. For the first time in all the long weary months of planning and working and striving he had recognition, he had men, and he had money. The total financial assets were twenty thousand marks. This was not enough to purchase the estate at Tegelen, but it would be enough for something smaller.

Again he made a trip to Venlo. The town was perfectly situated for his purpose. Three Dutch railroads and three German ones offered splendid communication. But no suitable place for building a seminary was available, and so his thoughts turned again to Tegelen. He looked up the register of landed property in Tegelen and discovered an estate that would be ideal for his purpose. The property in question was owned by a Mr. De Riyk. This man lived in a small villa in Steyl, on the bank of the Meuse River.

Father Janssen went to see the old gentleman and explained his need and desire to purchase. Mr. De Riyk not only refused to sell his property at Tegelen, but warned him that if he ever tried to buy anything in that district, he would have him for a competitor.

Father Janssen said nothing. What was there to say? At the very outset of his search for a site for the mission seminary he had entrusted the entire matter to a competent champion, an archangel. He had no fear of the outcome.

After some moments of reflection, Mr. De Riyk went on to say, "The property of Nicholas Ronck, however, is right near here, and it is for sale. Buy that. It has a fine location."

Father Janssen thanked him and went from the house. He walked down to the river. On the other bank stood the Ronck property. He walked over to a pier. The old ferryman, whose boat supplied the only means of communication between the two banks of the river, sat contentedly idle, puffing at his pipe. "What kind of a house is that over there?" asked Father Janssen, gesturing toward the Ronck property.

"That's the Ronck inn, Reverend Sir." He puffed at his pipe reflectively a moment. "Yes, Reverend Sir, the Ronck inn. And a lot of money has been made there in that inn, for many and many a year."

And then, with no further inducement, the old man launched into a long-winded recital of the former glories of Steyl, when as many as twenty freighters would be moored along its steep bank, their holds laden with coal, lime, timber, salt, foodstuff and other commodities, which would be unloaded and then transported deep inland, even as far as the Rhineland. Sailors and teamsters crowded the inn. The large warehouse would be packed high and deep with goods. And the little village was a beehive of business and barter, of comings and goings, with the inn as the center of it all.

But then the railroads had been built. The ship trade slowly diminished and died. Now quiet reigned at Steyl and at the inn. It wasn't much good any more, the inn, as a place of business. Not many people came this way any more. It was up for sale.

As the old man rattled on, a curious change come into the eyes of the priest. The alert interest seemed to dim out and take on the hazed look that comes with the memory of forgotten things. His thoughts roved fitfully, musingly over what the old man had been telling him and the scene outspread before him. Strange for him to have found this little harbor on a winding stream into whose sheltering banks had come ships from the seven seas, ships laden with riches from the orient and the far-off ends of the earth. It was as though his own ship of seeking had at last come to port. The little town had died. There were quicker means to get goods into the land, and its quiet little river would be disturbed no more by cargo-laden ships. Strange it would be were the town to revive and send forth from its banks cargo-laden ships to the orient and the far-off ends of the earth. This little town's life had been all a taking. In the miracle of time's revolving wheel it might yet become a new town with its life all a giving.

He smiled at the garrulous old man, gave him a tip, and was ferried across to the opposite bank.

He walked up to the inn and stared at the door. A smile broke the quiet of his face. Over the door hung a juniper bough — a proclamation that genuine gin was to be had at the bar.

The greenish-white house looked cheerful and attractive among the deep-foliaged chestnut trees; fresh green meadows stretched wide and free all about it. The sweeping graceful curves of the river made a large letter S as it cut its way through the soft fertile soil. It was idyllic; the land, the earth, the wide sky above, and the river sleeping beneath it.

He entered the inn and told the people that he was interested in buying the place. They offered him the entire property, one and one half acres, including the house, for a price that was within his means.

It seemed the answer to prayer, but he did not close with the offer. He wanted to have the opinion of others, so he merely took an option on the property for eight days.

The next week he returned to Steyl with two competent men who inspected the property for him. Both thought the place suitable and the price reasonable. The bill of purchase was made out that day. A few weeks later an adjacent warehouse was included in the purchase and on August 4, 1875, the entire property became his.

To make the transaction as secure as possible, Father Peter Bill, of Luxemburg, acquired Dutch citizenship, and the deed of ownership was made out to him. It seemed the only way to handle the matter at the moment, since Father Janssen's German citizenship might prove of need in their later conduct of the work. But with his usual long view of the matter, Father Janssen obtained a note from Father Bill, covering the full amount of the purchase.

108

As soon as the transaction was completed he hastened to share his own deep joy with the readers of his magazine: "With the help of God, a plot of ground and a dwelling place has at last been acquired for the mission enterprise. We hope and pray that the Lord will look graciously upon this new dwelling which is not destined for the pursuit of any common worldly interests, but for the highest aims here on earth. Here men shall be trained to be entirely devoted to God, with body and soul, with all their strength, to the last breath of life — men willing to follow in the footsteps of the Apostles; men who will not seek their own honor; men ready to sacrifice ease and comfort, even their own lives, in order to carry the light of Christ's teaching and the glory of God's name to all those nations that are still sitting in the darkness of spiritual death."

His words show the exuberance of his joy, the high flying banners of his sacred purpose, but then his native prudence and caution reasserts itself. There had been too much of trial and tribulation from the outset of this work not to realize that any success in it could come from God alone and the ones He inspired to help it: "May the Lord, who has given us the grace of making the decision and the start, not withhold from us the completion of the work. May He inspire pious people to help us with their prayers and alms; for, without their support, those who are to carry on the work will be powerless."

The mission seminary was to be dedicated on the 8th of September, the Nativity of the Blessed Virgin Mary. In preparation for it Father Janssen had written to Father Peter Bill, and the seminarians John Anzer and

109

Francis Reichart, asking them to dedicate themselves to the Sacred Heart in behalf of the new work. "The mission seminary," he explained, "has for its purpose to work for the realization of the intentions of the Sacred Heart. This dedication of ourselves to the Sacred Heart will be a lasting reminder of the purpose for which we started the work, and will justify us in taking for the seminary's motto: 'May the heart of Jesus live in the hearts of men!'"

Francis Reichart and a carpenter, Henry Erlemann, were the first inhabitants of the seminary. They tried to put the empty house into some kind of living condition. The juniper bough above the door was removed and a little cross put in its place. Neither of the men knew anything about cooking and they were profoundly grateful when quite unexpectedly an expert chef came to care for the commissary. This was a full-bearded Capuchin, Brother Juniper, who, for a number of years had been cook at the Capuchin monastery in Muenster. Brother Juniper was none other than William Janssen, Father Janssen's younger and jovial minded brother.

The Capuchins had just been placed under a decree of exile by the Prussian Government, and their members had been assigned by their superiors to various foreign monasteries. When Brother Juniper went to his Provincial and asked, "Where am I to go?" he received the reply: "You will go to your brother at Kempen and from there with him to Steyl. He wants to found a mission seminary and needs help. He wrote and asked as a favor that you should be allowed to assist him in this difficult period."

Brother Juniper did not like the idea. He would be obliged to lay aside his habit and wear civilian clothes.

110

He would have preferred to have gone to one of their monasteries in the Tirol or Holland, so that he could continue the regular life of a religious. But the Provincial had decided the matter, and so Brother Juniper set out for Kempen.

He arrived late at night and was received with open arms by his brother Arnold. He took him into his modest quarters and said to him: "Look, Brother, here is a fine glass of beer. I purposely saved it for you from last night."

"What! Stale beer!" Brother Juniper's eyebrows lifted in amazement. "Arnold, if it's all the same to you — I'll have a glass of water."

"It is still very good," protested Arnold. "I often save a glass of beer for the following day."

Brother Juniper did not appreciate this questionable charity, but he was considerably edified by a spirit so mortified that it could find stale beer "still very good."

Preparations were begun for the departure to Steyl.

When the final day arrived Father Boes of Kempen, dean of the clergy, held a little informal farewell celebration for Father Janssen. All the priests of the town were present. Although most of them considered the idea of the new foundation as rather visionary, yet all of them liked the unassuming priest who had lived in their midst these past years.

The farewell celebration was abundantly seasoned with jests, and the "itinerant apostle" was the butt of much teasing. They all agreed that his well-worn cassock and shabby hat would fit in well with the old inn at Steyl. They filled his glass and urged him to drink; it would be his last opportunity; on the Meuse there was nothing but water. Father Janssen laughed heartily and rejoiced in the cheer of the others.

111

One of the priests took out his pocketbook and poured all of its contents on the table. "Here, Arnold," he said, "this is for you and for your new mission seminary!" All the rest of the guests swiftly followed suit. The heaped up money made a generous farewell present, for which Father Janssen thanked them, in a voice husky with emotion.

The good people of Kempen, too, contributed their mite to help him. Some farmers offered to haul Father Janssen's furniture and books to Steyl. Brother Juniper went with them, and Father Janssen took the train to Kaldenkirchen, which was the last frontier station, and there waited for the wagons. From this place they made their entry into Steyl.

The first thing to do now was to prepare for the day of dedication. The joyful event was, of course, to be celebrated in a worthy manner. It was true that the house lacked almost everything, and the little household of four were not able to accomplish great things. However, the villagers went to work with great enthusiasm to supply suitable decorations. A large triumphal arch was erected, many wreaths were made to adorn the village church and the mission house, and numerous banners completed the decorations. A number of festively garlanded boards announced the character of the celebration. The one over the door of the parish church read: "Go ye into the whole world and preach the Gospel to every creature." Above the door of the house, where the juniper branch had been supplanted by the crucifix, the text ran: "Unless the Lord builds the house, they labor in vain that build it." In the vestibule one could read the words Father Janssen had decided upon as the seminary's motto: "May the heart

112

of Jesus live in the hearts of men!" and finally, in the dining room was found this text: "This is the victory which overcometh the world: our Faith."

The house was dedicated by a representative of Bishop Paeredis of Roermond. The Solemn High Mass was sung by Father von Essen, and Father Janssen delivered the sermon. His heart was full to overflowing, and he spoke at great length about the immense pagan countries, describing the plight of millions of souls, who, far from God, were doomed to the saddest of fates for time and eternity. He showed what had been done and was being done for their salvation — that it was far too little, that the Catholic Church was obliged to do more. "These considerations," he explained, "have moved us to attempt the founding of a mission seminary. The good God has helped us, and after many efforts we have made a modest beginning. God alone knows whether it will be a success. For the present, we thank the Giver of all good things for His assistance. Let us hope that this seminary will achieve its purpose. The poor and plain appearance of things at present should not discourage us. Even the greatest tree is at first only a tiny seed, and the strongest giant a weak and wailing babe. We are well aware that, with the present meager resources, we are not equal to our task; but we are confident that the good Lord will give us all that we need. His holy will be done. If something comes of this, we shall thank God; if nothing comes of it, we must humbly strike our breast and confess that we are not worthy of the grace."

At the frugal banquet twenty five guests were present. The good people of the village had loaned tables, chairs, linens, cutlery, for the occasion. In the midst of

the festivities letters of approbation were received from
several Bishops, and, to crown the joy of the day, a
telegram arrived from Rome with the apostolic blessing
for the opening of St. Michael's Mission Seminary.
True to his promise, Father Janssen had named the
seminary after the archangel who had helped him to
its realization.

For all its simplicity and poverty, the little house
meant a great deal to Father Janssen, and his cup of
happiness was filled to the brim. But his success in no
way changed his childlike faith. He told the readers of
his magazine all about the great day and concluded:
"Thus it has come about that the birthday of our Blessed
Mother has also become the birthday of our house.
May it never prove unworthy of its august protectress.
May the Mother of God continue to cast on this infant
institution a glance of motherly love. May it grow in
strength and by its good spirit deserve to become a
loved child of Mary."

Chapter 13

*I*T HAD been an auspicious beginning. Everything had gone off well. The start had at last been made.

But this was the day after. The townspeople had taken back the furniture and the articles which they had loaned for the dedication, and the interior of the house looked bleak and bare. Father Janssen walked from one empty room to the next and came at last to the vestibule. He stood there a moment, staring reflectively at the motto that hung there in solitary splendor. "May the heart of Jesus live in the hearts of men."

It came clearly to him in that moment that what he had done up till now was nothing. He had merely obtained the ground and the tools — now came the work and the ploughing. This house, that had been a tavern and was now a seminary, was a seminary only in name. It was fifty feet long and had two stories. There were five rooms on each floor and two somewhat roomy halls. These halls could be used as chapels.

He rolled up his sleeves, called his companions, and all of them set to work. The lower hall was soon a chapel. There was no altar, and there were no pews, only a picture of the Sacred Heart. But the hall had been swept clean and scrubbed, the windows were washed, and there were bunches of flowers in bottles before the picture. Here the members of the house could assemble for their morning and night prayers. They had to kneel on the stone floor, and Father Janssen's prayers usually lasted very long. A few days of this and Brother Juniper plaintively protested that it was rather rough on a man's knees to have to kneel so long on the cold stones. "Oh," replied Father Janssen, "that is all for the benefit of the poor pagans, Brother."

On the second floor they had arranged what was grandiloquently called: "St. Mary's Chapel." It was a simple pedestal, bearing a small statue of the Blessed Virgin, with two candles in front of it. After night prayers they all gathered here, the candles were lighted, and the "Hail, Holy Queen" was sung. That became the established way for them to end each day.

The furnishings of the new seminary and the mode of its inhabitants were even poorer than the outward appearance of the building would indicate. The day after the dedication Father Janssen had told some of his friends: "The house is paid for, but we begin our life here with an empty purse." It was no exaggeration.

The purchasing of the house and property had exhausted his funds, and he knew that to avoid debts the strictest economy would have to prevail. He himself was a man of frugal habits, and a great lover of poverty.

Although he dressed neatly, his clothes, well worn and carefully mended, were the occasion for many a humorous remark and even mild reproof from his friends. He never showed any resentment, but neither did he purchase better looking clothes. The poverty of his new home in no way disconcerted him. Actually he seemed glad that it lacked even the essentials for ordinary comfort, and he assured his co-workers time and again that the poverty of the place would draw down God's special blessing on their work.

All of them slept on straw sacks until Henry Erlemann by slow degrees built bedsteads for them. Father Janssen slept on the floor longest of all, because he would not use a bedstead until the last of his companions had been taken care of. When his turn finally arrived he ordered the carpenter to make one with a lid on it, so it would serve in the daytime as a table!

For quite some time there were only four chairs for the five members of the house. During meals, two of the chairs were placed somewhat close together and a board was laid over them. By that arrangement three were seated instead of two.

A few weeks after the dedication, four German priests called on Father Janssen. Jokingly they inquired when St. Michael's Mission Seminary would send its first missionaries to China. He took their chaffing good-naturedly. Later on when the visitors were having some refreshments, he poured the coffee for them and served their needs, standing. Repeatedly they requested him to sit down with them. Finally he was obliged to admit that there was not another chair in the house. That put an end to the joking. A few days later a dozen chairs arrived as a contribution from his visitors.

117

Bowls, plates and drinking cups were ordered from an earthenware dealer in the neighborhood. The heavy, unwieldy, dull-colored crockery was not exactly a representative specimen of the ceramic art, but it was cheap and durable.

Bed linen was scarce. For every new arrival, material for a new straw sack was the first thing to be bought. Father Janssen always purchased very economically, and would give the exact measurement of the various pieces that had to be made. On one occasion, a number of large bed sheets were donated, and he thriftily had them cut in two. Then he discovered that they were too small, and while they would cover a straw sack mattress they would not stay in place. So he ordered them sewed down to the beds. This appeared to him in the light of a very useful discovery, and the practice was kept up for some time.

The laundry and mending were done by some girls from the neighborhood.

What caused Father Janssen no small concern was the problem of securing the necessary food. The people of the village had provided him, during the first weeks, with potatoes and vegetables. There were also benefactors from the neighboring town of Venlo who had helped substantially. But winter was at hand and they needed a supply of food. Father Janssen talked the matter over with his brother. Brother Juniper had had experience in collecting alms for his order, but to beg for alms at that time was prohibited by law. The need of the seminary was so great, however, that Brother Juniper was quite ready to chance a begging tour.

His first attempt was made at Straelen. The parish priest was willing to help him. He took him to one of his parishioners, a farmer, and had just completed the introductions and explanations, when a policeman entered the house. The farmer had enough presence of mind to invite the guardian of the law to have coffee. The policeman sat down next to Brother Juniper and the two men conversed very freely with each other.

Twice that same afternoon, at different farms, the policeman met Brother Juniper and each time he eyed the bushily bearded stranger with a steadily growing suspicion.

That evening the information reached the rectory that, in a meeting of the village council, it had been reported a disguised monk was going through the town begging the people for alms. This was an infringement of the law, and the council had issued orders for the police to arrest the dangerous individual the following day.

When the police arrived next morning at the rectory the man behind the whiskers had already fled across the border.

Brother Juniper's failure was quite a disappointment to Father Janssen. But some days later a wagon drew up before the seminary door. Two farmers dismounted and unloaded thirty bushels of potatoes. They told Father Janssen that they were from Straelen. They had heard that a religious, asking alms, had been chased out of their parish by the police. Filled with honest indignation they had loaded their wagon with potatoes, and here it was: "Just for spite!"

Another begging tour at Kempen was so successful that for several months no further attempts were necessary.

Brother Juniper made many more trips, and his sunny disposition and grand sense of humor made a host of friends for the seminary. But he was not alone in that important task.

The *Little Messenger of the Sacred Heart* also did its share in winning friends and benefactors and new applicants for the little seminary at Steyl. It was still printed at Paderborn. When the bundles of copies arrived each month at the railroad station in Kaldenkirchen, the entire household went there, and, in a rented room, did the packing and shipping.

The great distance, however, between the place of printing and shipping caused such difficulty, that before long, Father Janssen purchased a hand press, and began to print the magazine at Steyl.

They still had, however, to transport the magazine to Kaldenkirchen for shipping. At first the students themselves pulled the wagon. Later on they borrowed a neighbor's dog cart.

The little seminary had two priests, but no altar. An old altar had been donated by a parish and shipped to Kaldenkirchen, but the problem of having it hauled out to Steyl seemed insurmountable. A teamster, Mr. Spee, heard of their difficulty and transported the altar, free of charge, to the seminary. When he learned of their monthly trips with the magazine he volunteered to take that chore off their shoulders. For several years this kindly man did all the trucking for them gratis.

It was the charity of the poor that made possible the start as well as the development of the mission seminary. Father Janssen was profoundly aware of that and just as profoundly grateful for it. And at the first

120

opportunity he publicized that fact in his magazine: "Until now the good God has helped our little mission house especially through the gifts of the poor; and we are grateful for that, because these are the gifts on which the greatest blessing rests. May they help us to become truly poor in spirit, for of such is the Kingdom of God. Money, though we need it badly, is our least concern. The Lord has said, 'Seek ye first the Kingdom of God, and his justice, and all these things shall be added unto you.' These words apply, above all, to a house like ours. Therefore we beg Him unceasingly, through the patrons of the house, to make us good and devout, and also to send us good and devout people to be co-workers with us in His vineyard."

These lines reveal clearly the spirit in which Father Janssen was trying to carry on his work, and the spirit with which he was trying to imbue his followers. In every possible manner, he tried to cultivate in them the spirit of prayer. On the very day of his arrival in Steyl he set up the order of prayers that were to be recited daily. Among them was one that was to be repeated every fifteen minutes, at the stroke of the clock. It consisted of short alternating acts of faith, hope, and charity, contrition, and spiritual communion. It was called the Quarter Hour Prayer, and everyone in the house had to say it. When several were together in one room, the oldest in age had to lead. And the prayer was said no matter what type of work they might be engaged in at the moment.

To frequent prayers were added acts of mortification. The poverty of those first days offered many opportunities for it, and he himself was an example for all of them. He seemed to have fewer needs than anybody else in the house, and that made it easier for the others to put up with the absence of many things that they might ordinarily have expected. They learned to get along with little and feel happy in their poverty. He made it a point to acknowledge gratefully every alms, every little help given the house, and to see that it was used economically.

But for Father Janssen there were other things besides this care to imbue his followers with a deeply religious spirit. There were a host of material cares, the hard facts of dollars and cents, of housing and food, of a magazine and benefactors, of letters and ways and means to arouse the interest of people. Arousing interest in the missions was a pioneering project. He was attempting to move an almost completely inert mass and the weight of its inertness was at times discouragingly evident. Since boyhood he had had a deep awareness of the strange mystery and tragedy of the light and the darkness. It had come to him out of the sublime prologue to St. John's Gospel: "In the beginning was the Word ... and the Word was God.... It was the true light which enlightens every man who comes into the world" (Jo. 1, 9). Light shining in darkness. That Light was the Word, the Divine Word, the Eternal Word, God — "and the world knew It not."

The poignancy of that most tragic of all the world's tragedies had driven deep into his soul and stayed there unvoiced, unexpressed, like a deep wound of desire, widening, growing because it had no way to relieve its pent up longing save by the outpouring of prayer.

The Word is to most people an abstraction, but to the simple mind of Arnold's father it had always been a great Reality. And he, too, had learned to know the Word as such. It was a Person, this Word, an Eternal Word which the Eternal Mind of the Father had eternally spoken. And, as a word spoken by a man mirrors that man's mind, so the Eternal Word was a flawless mirror of the mind of God, a perfect likeness of all the beauty and goodness and greatness that is God. But the wonder and the mystery of it was that the Divine Word was not just a likeness of God, *It was God,* the great God, who created all the marvels of sky and field, of earth and stream, who peopled with beauty and splendor all the depths of the sea, and the expanses of earth, and, who, with gentle omnipotence, kept all these wonders in existence for the children of men. This the Divine Word had done. The Word spoken by the Father. The Son begotten eternally by the Father. The Son of God had done these things for the sons of men.

And in the fulness of time that overwhelming love of the Divine Word had come even closer to men. It had stooped from the ineffable heights of the divinity and become man. "And the Word was made flesh." The Divine Word took to Himself a human body with a human heart filled to overflowing with love for the Father, and with love for His lost children. He had come to save. For men, who had lost the way, He would be the way; for men, who had forgotten the true language, He would speak; for the wordlessness of our misery He would be the Word, the Word that would not only express to us all the love and beauty and compassion of the Father for us, but also would be the Word expressing to the Father all our needs, our dependence, our trust and faith. In that one Word all of

123

God had been and is eternally expressed, and in that one Word all of mankind finds voice. For that Word is our prayer and its answer, our plea and fulfillment, our hope and salvation in time and eternity.

And in that Incarnate Word there dwelt the tenderest, most loving of human hearts, a heart that was filled with a burning desire for the love of men, a heart that was saddened unutterably with man's rejection. He had "come into his own and his own received him not ...!"

This was the tragedy that burned deeply and darkly in Father Janssen's soul. The tragedy of Divinity rejected. The tragedy of Love that loved the unloving. And the darkness of mankind's rejection somehow shadowed his own soul and always would. For we are all members of one family, and the greatness and littleness of each member reflects on all the rest of us, for good or for evil, for greatness or littleness. But the sorrow of that fact has, too, its joy; "to such as received Him he gave the power to be sons of God," and being His son had joy untold in it. It carried too a responsibility: to bring back the erring ones to the Father, to carry to the darkness the light, to the unloved the Love, to those whose ears were deafened with the shrill cries of greed and misery and loss the great peace of the Word.

Father Janssen had been in the world. From the quiet of the farm he had come to the noise of the city. There he had heard many words spoken, but there was only one Word that made sense. So many had heard that Word and had closed their ears to it. There were so many millions who as yet had not heard of It, and it had been the desire of the great Heart of Christ that the Word be spread to all, through the ministry of men. It had been the desire of the Divine Word that as He had done, so should men do, becoming a word of glad tidings, bringing the knowledge of Him, the Eternal Word, to others.

And so the Divine Word became Father Janssen's book of life. What the Divine Word desired had become the one goal of his life, and all the desires, the affections, the great hopes of the Divine Word were contained in the Heart of Christ. During his early years of priesthood he had labored for the fulfillment of them, and by slow sure means he had been led to the place and position where he could bring to realization a work that would be actively directed toward that aim.

A month before St. Michael's Mission Seminary had come into existence he had put himself and his enterprise under the protection of the Divine Word. Dimly he had grasped, at that time already, some of the difficulties and needs that the work entailed. He had called upon the Divine Word as the Eternal Wisdom, the Image of the Father, the Sender of the Holy Spirit, as the Light that enlightens every man who comes into the world. He had prayed that the "Divine Word might be the soul of our devotion, our strength, our love and our light. From Him may our teachers learn the wisdom, and our missionaries find the words of eloquence with which to establish the Kingdom of God in the night of heathenism, in the cold and dreary kingdom of the evil spirit."

With deep and farseeing purposefulness he had gone from the very outset of his venture to the ultimate Reality as a basis. He had founded the enterprise on rock, the unshakable fastness of a divine intent — to work for God, and through God to find for his followers

125

the divine wisdom and eloquence that alone could achieve real results.

He singled out the Second Person of the Trinity, the Divine Word, for special adoration, because "He is the person of our Divine Savior, whose brothers we became by sanctifying grace, whom we in our apostolate must follow along the path of abandonment to God. He is the Light that enlightens every man, and in Him the missionary must put his trust, knowing that his words will have true efficacy only through the assistance of the Divine Word, who brought forth heaven and earth out of nothing. He is the uncreated Wisdom, from whom all human wisdom proceeds, and therefore He is deserving of special veneration by our teachers."

His ruling purpose in starting the seminary was that the light of faith might be brought to the darkness of unbelief. They were to preach the word of God, and it would have to be the Word of God that would make their efforts fruitful. "The preaching of the faith can bear fruit only through the grace of the Divine Word, who enlightens every man who comes into the world."

All these thoughts he had condensed into a single phrase, that was both a challenge, a crusading cry, and an humble prayer: "May the Heart of Jesus live in the hearts of men, and may the Sweet Light of the Divine Word shine in the darkness of sin and in the night of heathenism."

His aims were lofty, the means to fulfill them lowly. Many an hour, in quiet meditation, he pondered them, during this period when the work was scraping along from day to day on the charity of the poor.

The world has no recognition for that which is small and poor. And the little seminary at Steyl was small

126

and poor, indeed. The prevailing opinion in Germany was that Father Janssen's work had no prospects of success. It was not only the educated laity that held that opinion, but also the clergy. They pointed out that the enterprise had no solid financial backing, as was evidenced by is tawdry sort of location and house. They particularly called attention to the individuals who were at the head of the venture, as proof that the whole thing was foredoomed to failure.

Father Janssen was well aware of this pessimistic attitude. Its repercussions fell upon him personally. Almost everywhere he was received with suspicion, as a man of unsound ideas; and some judged him even more harshly. It was the general opinion that the whole venture would very quickly fall apart at the seams.

Most of the educated Hollanders shared the opinion held in Germany. One of the neighboring pastors openly stated: "Father Janssen thinks this mission seminary project is possible; but no one will ever see it succeed."

The townspeople of Tegelen prophesied that the undertaking would end in bankruptcy, and that the foolhardy Germans would soon return home.

It was a burden that was hard for Father Janssen to bear. Viewed from a business standpoint, he knew that the project did look hopeless. But as a religious work, undertaken for the glory of God, it was an honest attempt to meet a real need. Having the approbation of the hierarchy and the blessing of the Holy Father, he felt that it should have received the active support of all sincere Christians. But, for a long time, large Catholic circles showed no interest.

127

One of the things that he found very hard to understand was the attitude of the *Catholic Missions,* Germany's most influential mission magazine. For many years it failed to make any mention of his work. It refused to accept notices of activities at the mission house. When eventually it did condescend to make reference to the Steyl project, it was done in the fewest possible lines.

The impression created among the readers of the magazine was that this first German Mission Seminary did not deserve recognition and support.

Unfriendliness of this sort impeded the development of Father Janssen's work, but it did not prevent it. It only deepened his faith and turned Him more trustingly toward the Source of unfailing strength

Chapter 14

I T IS not too difficult a matter to face up to opposition, criticism, and to lack of material support when one has staunch friends at one's side. And there were such friends at Father Janssen's side, four of them, imbued with the same great zeal as he had for the cause of the foreign missions: Father von Essen, Father Peter Bill, the seminarians Francis Reichart and John Anzer. Of these four, one of them, Father von Essen, by force of circumstances, was compelled to remain in Germany. The other three, Father Bill, Reichart and Anzer, lived with him in the new mission seminary at Steyl. It was a well-balanced group. Two of them were priests, mature, devout, energetic. The other two were seminarians, young, eager, enthusiastic.

Father Janssen looked on these three as co-founders and called them that. They were completely one in their purpose to found a seminary for training foreign missionaries, and Father Janssen had promised them that when the time came to formulate the statutes for

129

their way of living, it would be done in consultation with them.

There were seminaries similar to theirs in other countries, and they knew that these seminaries differed rather widely in their statutes and methods of operation. The one in England, Mill Hill, had a much more stable organization and a more monastic character than the one in France, the Paris Foreign Mission Society. They were not decided which of these two would be the model for their own seminary at Steyl.

In a meeting on August 5, 1875, they agreed to ask Bishop Paredis to appoint Father Janssen as the provisional superior of the house. A permanent superior was to be elected after the statutes had been definitely formulated. Bishop Paredis acceded to their request, and Father Janssen was officially established as rector of the new seminary at Steyl.

At the same meeting Father Janssen read off to the other three men a preliminary draft of what was to be the scope and purpose of the work they were to engage in. It was meant to be the first step in giving their enterprise a more definite character and aim, so that their followers could start functioning as a definite organization. This preliminary draft was clear, simple and practical: "Our general aim is the service of God and our neighbor by spreading the knowledge and love of the Blessed Trinity. . . .

"Of the three Divine Persons, we wish to worship in particular the Divine Word who dwells in our midst in the tabernacle. . . .

"Our special aims are: First — the propagation of the faith in pagan countries. Second — the cultivation

130

of true science (theology and the natural sciences) in the spirit of St. Thomas Aquinas. The second aim supplements the first.

"Our seminary, therefore, is to be open to the working out of this double purpose — that is, to those who wish to become missionaries, and to those who, as teachers, are ready to devote themselves to the instruction of the former. Over and above these special purposes, we shall do what we can for the glory of God and the benefit of the faithful by preaching and writing.

"To accomplish these things more effectively we choose for our institute the following patrons: The Blessed Virgin Mary, St. Joseph and St. Ann, the Holy Archangels (especially Michael, Gabriel and Raphael).

"Since our house, on account of the unfavorable conditions of the time, will not have any religious vows, it will be left to the individual members to determine what means they wish to employ to dedicate themselves to the Sacred Heart of Jesus; but it is desirable that all should adopt the third rule of St. Dominic."

There was, too, a regulation which specified that members were to retain possession of all money or property that was theirs, but were not to handle money directly.

In the discussion that followed, two points were rather strongly opposed by Father Bill and Francis Reichart. The first was that which represented the cultivation of science as one of the special aims of the institute. It plainly indicated that the teachers were to form a special group, and the members who were to go to the missions another. It seemed to them that the cultivation of science, in so far as it was necessary for the training of the missionaries, should be taken as a matter of course. It did not deserve the special emphasis he had placed upon it.

Still greater objection was taken to membership in the Third Order of St. Dominic. That required among other things, one day of fasting and four days of abstinence each week. Father Bill bluntly wanted to know who was going to observe all that fasting and abstinence. Certainly not the young students. And in clerical seminaries professors were usually dispensed from fasting, on account of their strenuous activities. In the missions themselves, the missionaries would have to eat what they could get, and should not be subjected to such regulations. In short, this rule would become the source of many exceptions and much discontent.

Father Janssen obtained the rules of various congregations and studied them carefully. It only confirmed him in his opinion that the rule of the Third Order of St. Dominic was the most practical one for their purpose.

Father Bill was older than Father Janssen, he had had a much wider experience in pastoral work, and his practical view of the matter easily drew the two seminarians to his side. The three of them told Father Janssen, in plain terms, in their meetings and discussions on the matter, that the two points he held to so insistently, the cultivation of the sciences and adoption of the rule of the Third Order of St. Dominic, were irreconcilable with the missionary purpose of the enterprise. Missionary work among the pagans should be designated as the sole purpose of the Society, and every other task should be expressly excluded. Every member should devote himself to this one purpose, and in the same manner. For a rule they should use the tried and tested constitutions of the Paris Foreign Missionary Society or the Mill Hill Fathers, and not the rule of the Dominicans.

They wanted an early settlement of this matter. They felt it was essential to have the framework of their organization swiftly and definitely laid. They called for a vote on the matter. But Father Janssen would not hear of that. He could not see the wisdom of putting so important an issue to a vote at this early stage of the proceedings. Two of the group, moreover, were young men who could scarcely be expected to judge wisely. He firmly stood for postponing the final settlement to a later date. That merely aggravated the others.

What started out as a mere divergence of opinion developed into a deep-rooted dissension that grew by leaps and bounds over the following six months. The core of the whole matter seemed to be that Father Bill, and the two seminarians who had lined themselves up in his camp, wished the new seminary to be an association of secular priests who would do foreign missionary work. Father Janssen, on the other hand, by his un-wavering adherence to the two moot points seemed bent on founding a religious order.

There is no indication that Father Janssen ever had such an idea. On the contrary, his proposal to have the members retain their money evidences that he had no thought of a religious order. There was to be in the group not a vow of poverty but a deep spirit of poverty.

That a conflict of opinions should have arisen is not to be wondered at. These men were all positive personalities. Eager, capable and fired with a high purpose. Each of them saw the fulfillment of that purpose in his own way, according to his own personality and mental outlook. Evil men disagree violently about the attainment of their aims, from low motives of greed and selfish advancement. Good men, too, can disagree about the attainment of their high purposes and from the highest of motives. And these were good men.

But the surprising thing in this conflict is the emergence of an unsuspected facet in the character of Father Janssen. By nature he was frail of health and shy in comportment. There was nothing of aggressiveness about him. If there had been his previous ventures might have gotten much further than they did. He was slow, cautious, hesitating. Everyone knew that. His associates better than the rest. But they had not imagined him to be so strong-willed, so hard to sway. Always there had been in him a certain attitude of awe, almost of timidity, when dealing with priestly confreres, especially those who had something of a reputation for ability or learning. It was the result of his earliest days at school when even his best friends had made little of his mental attainments, despite his undoubted mathematical and scientific talents. Humbly he took their estimate for granted.

Now for the first time that attitude changes. He stands up to them, opposes them, and is as immovable as rock.

It is a startling change, and one that leaves his associates irritated and completely bewildered. That curious and unexpected side of him was to bewilder more than one person in the course of his life. And yet it had a very simple basis. He was timid before men, but not when God's interests were concerned. When the Will of God was manifest to him then all his ineptness,

134

his sense of inferiority fell away. There was only one course of action open to him — to do that Divine Will, despite the opposition, criticism, and slights of men, who, by talent and training, the world would say were more mature and capable of judging. He had to obey God in the first place. There was no longer any timidity or shyness in the presence of others then, be they learned, or in the highest position.

What his associates did not grasp throughout this conflict was that this unrelenting attitude of his toward the entire point of controversy was a firmness of will that was not of nature but of grace.

From early days he had allowed things to approach him as the designs of God arranged them. By prayer and quiet thought he tried to come to God's intention. When he thought he saw it clearly, he set about carrying it out, firmly, persistently, completely. His guiding star was a single, unmoving star, the Will of God. And this Divine Will would be manifested by the voice of authority. In the letter which he and Father von Essen had drawn up for the Archbishop of Cologne, the scope of the work had been outlined. It had been stated therein that, as a secondary purpose, the seminary should cultivate the sciences, and that the personnel of the seminary should practice the rule of the Third Order of St. Dominic. The Archbishop of Cologne had given his official approval to that document, and the scholarly Bishop Haneberg of Speyer had, in particular, warmly recommended the cultivation of the sciences in connection with missionary activities.

That Father Janssen should look for a solid religious basis for the new seminary was elementary prudence and sound procedure. That he should, in order to avoid mistakes and long experimenting, adopt a mode of life tested by many centuries, was good judgment. He chose the rule of the Third Order of St. Dominic, because the Dominicans seemed to combine, in a most happy manner, the preaching of the word of God with a life of penance.

He had used all human means to discover the Will of God and this seemed to be it. The voice of authority had spoken in favor of it. He followed it as such, but he listened painstakingly to all the reasons brought forward by the others, and in none of them found reason to change.

The argument developed into a series of unending discussions. Repeatedly, to obtain dispassionate judgments in the matter, Father Janssen had each of them put down his views and arguments in writing. It was all to no avail. The entire situation merely deteriorated. Father Bill and the seminarians, irritated by Father Janssen's refusal to give in to their views, began to doubt his ability to be the head of their project, and the more they doubted, the more his authority suffered. They decided that he had no talent for organization, that he was stubborn, that he would not take advice. They themselves had enlisted the opinions of more than one person outside of their seminary and they alleged the agreement of these other people as a proof for the the correctness of their views. The weight of opposition against Father Janssen grew daily heavier and heavier.

Father Janssen lost much weight, he grew ill. Many a time he asked: "O Lord, how can this work succeed?" He knew that with no unity in the minds and hearts of his co-founders nothing could be achieved. Father

Bill was a goodhearted man, but he did not grasp the full scope of what this work was to mean; the two clerics were young, impressionable, and outside influence had swayed them. They were all three very dear to him, and it cut him to the quick to see their growing coldness toward him, their increasing hostility to the ideas that he had so unbendingly to adhere to. Young Reichart was especially dear to him and he had said to him: "I have been thinking that the Lord could not punish me more severely than by your going away. Let us both pray to the Sacred Heart that this will never happen." But Reichart answered that he could give no promise, that he did not know if he would remain.

The others in the household knew nothing of all this dissension, but it was evident to Brother Juniper that Arnold was burdened with some great trial and care. And one day when Arnold looked more ill than usual he pressed him for an explanation, and the over-burdened priest's dam of self-reserve broke, and he wept unrestrainedly. But the words that he spoke, under the excess of his grief, were only a vague hint as to the source of his trial.

He had granted concessions, as far as he could; he had promised the other three that he would not found a Dominican congregation, that he would not introduce the habit of the Dominicans, but would use the cassock of the secular priests, that he would mitigate the mortification of the rule of the Third Order. But they did not want mitigations, they wanted capitulation.

Despite all these things he would not be turned from his original purpose. It was then that Father Bill, under the advice of some misguided friends, decided to force Father Janssen to capitulate. He had a weapon to hand

137

for that task. He was the legal owner of the house and property.

Father Janssen suddenly found himself in the unhappy position of the three others going on with the work along the lines they had decided upon, and leaving him outside. All efforts to make Father Bill transfer the title of the house to himself were fruitless. Father Janssen was the acting superior of the seminary, he had gathered the money which had been paid for the house, and yet he was in danger of their proceeding without him.

In his need he went to the Bishops of Roermond and Luxemburg, laid the matter before them, showed them the note which Father Bill had given him at the time the house was purchased and invoked their aid. The Bishops sided with him and compelled Father Bill to hand over to him the title.

Father Janssen describes the event in the following words: "I had begged and implored Father Bill, but in vain. Then during the afternoon, when the first vespers of the Feast of the Annunciation began, he capitulated. This consoled me very much because I had been thinking of giving the Society the name — Society of the Divine Word."

All the men concerned in this dissension were undoubtedly sincere. "None of us three," declared Father Bill, "wanted to remove Father Janssen, least of all did I. Though I believed his plans were impracticable under the circumstances, I thought that they might become possible later ..., we did not intend to destroy his work, but simply to carry out the original plan of a German missionary society either with him, or if that proved impossible, without him." The sincerity of their intentions had dictated the course of action that seemed right and justifiable to each of them. But the rift that had appeared in their group had now grown so deep and wide that it was impossible of healing. Both Father Bill and Mr. Reichart left the seminary.

Father Janssen walked with the two all the way to the railroad station at Kaldenkirchen. He carried Father Bill's traveling bag. All of them were depressed, and heavy of heart. Repeatedly Father Janssen asked Father Bill if he would not stay, if there were not some way that they could reach an agreement. There was one way, but it was an impossible way, because it meant that Father Janssen would have to give up his plans to theirs.

So they parted sadly, quietly. Father Bill carried with him a letter of highest recommendation from Father Janssen which explained his departure from the seminary was due to the fact that their views about the character of the mission seminary were too divergent.

Father Janssen walked back alone, and going through the village of Steyl he passed some groups of people who looked on him with respectful yet pitying eyes. They had witnessed the departure of the others, and the news had spread that the men had left permanently. He walked past them and heard their comments when they thought him out of hearing. "That is the end of the whole business. The mission seminary is finished."

A short while later Father von Essen also withdrew from his association with Steyl. Anzer alone remained and he was so completely unsettled by the whole dissension that it seemed but a matter of a short while before he, too, would go.

During these critical days, when three of his co-workers left him, there was scarcely anyone who had any vestige of belief in the success of the seminary. Many considered Father Janssen himself the greatest obstacle to its success. They called him incapable, eccentric, and stubborn.

None of them knew what had gone on in this silent man's heart during these days of trial. At the height of all the trouble, before his appeal to the Bishop, he had spoken to Brother Juniper: "Now it will become manifest whether the work is from God; if it is not, let it break up now. If that is the Will of God, I am content. If that is His Will then it were better for matters to come to a head today than tomorrow. I have only had God in mind."

Out of the depth of his heart those words had come, in simplicity and truth. It was only God's Will that he had sought, and God's Will had stripped from him everyone. He had a mission seminary, but no men. He had made a struggling start and this was the end. He was alone. What had happened was God's Will. Why? To what end? He did not know. What was to follow he did not know. So he would stay on here till that Will showed its design.

Chapter 15

A MAN that is single-minded is as a rule easily satisfied. There is only one thing that interests him, and in the pursuit of that one object he finds release for his energies and freedom from the envies and restlessness of those whose minds and hearts are set on a multiplicity of desires. Such a man is a happy man. He is never at a loss what to do, never cast into a period of despondency by temporary setbacks. He desires only one thing. If setbacks, temporary failures befall him they only serve to send him off on some other track in pursuit of his one and only objective. His singleness of purpose is his salvation, his great blessing.

But there is another aspect, too, to the matter. When complete failure comes to such a man then his whole world ends. He had only one thing he desired. The complete frustration of that desire puts an end to all purpose for his life.

Father Janssen had worked with complete absorption for a single idea — the founding of a mission

141

seminary. He had the realization of that goal in his hands, and then it had all crumbled away into failure. This was not a temporary setback, it was complete failure. It was not merely that the men had gone from him, that he stood alone — there was the very clear realization of what their defection would mean. The story of the conflict would be spread abroad. There would be news value in the fact that the new enterprise had died a-borning. What mattered it that the Bishops had sided with him, that the building and the lands were now in his possession? The men who had left were not malicious. He knew that. He would defend their characters, the purity of their motives, and their piety before anyone. But they would be asked to give their version of the story, and he knew how he had appeared these last weeks in their eyes. Despite their fairness he would seem impractical, slow and stubborn. And the prospect of such a man acting as the rector of the seminary would kill the desire of any priests or seminarians to enter the mission seminary.

He had had one simple goal — to found a mission seminary — and that was now ended. His whole world would have ended if that had been the extent of his simplicity. But the oneness of view in his sturdy soul reached much deeper and wider. He had "only God in mind," and so nothing ended, except a phase in his life, the work that he had thought was God's Will to be done. His simplicity had not changed. It endured and supported him. He had said that "if the work was not God's then it is better that it break up now," and it had broken up. He was left in an empty shell, an untenanted house, and land that was not peopled. His purpose still remained — to do God's Will, and what that

Will was he did not know. So he stayed silently there, alone, praying and waiting.

To a priest friend he wrote and detailed the main events of this sad time: "It is a heavy blow," he concluded, "and all the more so since Anzer, the other seminarian, is also affected ... *In Cruce Salus!* I am glad that I was forced to drink from the cup of suffering of the Lord.... *L'union fait la force* (In union there is strength), and for that reason our aim could not have been reached with the men we have had with us up to this time. But I am alone, now, and you can imagine that I sometimes lose courage. May God's holy Will be done. If it is not His work, let it perish, the sooner the better."

Despite his sorrow and sense of aloneness he saw in his sudden collapse of the whole enterprise not only the design of God toward the seminary but a personal purpose toward himself. "Man, because of the deep corruption into which he has fallen, cannot be freed of his secret faults without suffering. Therefore I trust in God and ask Him to take my hand and guide me."

And he did that, fully, wholeheartedly, with all the thoroughness of his simple heart. And it was out of that experience that he was able to write: "He who loves God trusts Him. He who does not trust Him does not love Him. God cannot possibly betray our trust. We must let Him lead us by the hand as little children.... It is His way to make His intentions known to us only gradually at first. How else could we learn to walk before Him in the light of faith and of unconditional trust? The more adverse our circumstances, the more firm our trust must be. You know how highly St.

143

Francis Xavier esteemed confidence in God, and how he instilled it into his fellow-missioners. Let us thank God for all suffering! For how shall virtue become manly and resolute unless it be made so by suffering? Let us then place our trust in the wise direction of Divine Providence even in our darkest days."

His confidence was soon rewarded. John Anzer decided to remain. The unfortunate outcome of the long drawn out discussion had, of course, seriously upset him. He was by nature a generous-souled young man, filled with all the eagerness and fire of a high purpose. It had been disillusioning to witness how the human element can shipwreck a lofty purpose. He himself had had a part in the conflict, for he, no less than the others, was vitally concerned with the work that the seminary intended to perform. His love for the foreign missions was something really deep and truly apostolic, and it was that love which had led him to take an outspoken part in the conflict. It was a love that was so supernaturally great that it could lift him above personal convictions. The chief aim of the seminary was the work of the foreign missions. That, after all, was the one thing that mattered. The secondary purpose, which Father Janssen insisted be also included in the seminary's scope of endeavor, did not accord with his views. He never fully assented to it. But the essential thing was that this institution, which would work primarily for the foreign missions, should not be allowed to die. He signified his decision to Father Janssen. He would remain with him.

During May and June of 1876 the two men had a number of talks to determine the rules and regulations that were to guide them. Father Janssen's original outline of statutes, which had been the cause of the dissension, was again discussed, and, after several changes, it was decided that they would give it the test of practical use. On June 15 both signed their names to it.

The name of the Society was to be the *Societas Verbi Divini* (Society of the Divine Word), and the members were to venerate in a special manner the Divine Word and the Sacred Heart of Jesus.

They were to use the cassock of the secular clergy and the inner lining of the cincture was to be red "in memory of the love of the Sacred Heart of Jesus, of the blood He shed for us, and as a reminder that every member should be ready to shed his own blood as a martyr for the faith."

A special chapter was devoted to the spirit of the Society which was to be one of complete abandonment to God, a spirit of faith, confidence, humility and self-denial.

No ecclesiastical approbation was sought for these regulations. The general approbation given by the Bishops for founding the seminary was judged sufficient for the time being. They would have a freer hand that way to test out their regulations by actual experience and see what would be the best form of organization eventually for the work.

The decision of John Anzer, despite his failure to fully agree with him on the scope of the Society, was the first rift in a world that had been singularly dark and clouded. His confidence in God had not been in vain; the hand that he had placed so confidently in the Father's clasp was firmly held, and he was drawn quietly and quickly and surely into brighter ways.

Two co-workers had left the seminary, and now two new ones came in their stead. John Janssen, his youngest brother, and Hermann Wegener applied for admittance and were readily received. Both of these young men had finished their theological studies, and were deacons. Along with John Anzer they were ordained that same year.

What had seemed for Father Janssen the end of his work suddenly took on the appearance of merely the darkness before dawn. The first year of the seminary's existence was ended and he had three young priests at his side. He felt able now to go ahead more fully with the wider plans he had cherished for the work inside the seminary.

It had not been his purpose to found a seminary exclusively for philosophical and theological studies. He had also had in view something along the lines of what is called today a preparatory seminary. He visioned the seminary as a complete training course for missionaries, from their boyhood years through college and the seminary. To his mind a missionary needed other knowledge and more varied accomplishments than the priests who labored at home. A missionary had to be trained to greater readiness and deeper thoroughness in the spirit of generosity and sacrifice in order to persevere and meet effectively the demands of his difficult vocation.

His inauguration of this school at Steyl was a complete and quick success. The number of students increased rapidly. The prospect of study, work, prayer as the preparation for the life of an apostle in far-off lands seemed strangely attractive to youth.

Many young priests, deprived of priestly work by the persecution, came to Steyl, and acted as teachers for these students. Not all of them identified themselves with the Society. Most of them merely engaged to act as teachers on a temporary basis, but their assistance was invaluable.

And so the year which had begun so dismally ended on a note of joy. For to top all these actual signs of growth, the annual Convention of German Catholics at Munich issued a public recommendation of the new seminary at Steyl.

Chapter 16

S EVERAL YEARS before the work at Steyl started Father Janssen had been summoned to the deathbed of his father. With the rest of his family he had stood sorrowfully at the bedside of the old man and received from him his last legacy. Gerard Janssen had little of earthly goods to give his children, but from all of them he exacted a promise that when he was gone they would attend Mass each Sunday to thank the Blessed Trinity for the graces received during the past week; that they would hear Mass on Monday in honor of the Holy Ghost to implore His blessing for the new week. That had been his legacy to all of them. It was the last act of a father to keep his family one, united. It was the deepest and dearest treasure that he had gained from a life of work and striving and prayer.

Father Arnold brought Viaticum, and as the end of life drew near he asked his dying parent if there was any fear about the approaching end. His father had replied with simple faith. "No. God is with me. Of what should I be afraid?"

He slipped away from them quietly. A good, simple, strong man, filled with the goodness and simplicity and strength of the One whom he had loved and in whose ways he had walked.

Arnold never forgot that promise made to his dying father. His Mass on Sundays was an act of thanksgiving to the Trinity for the graces of the past week; his Mass on Mondays, a petition to the Holy Spirit to bless the forthcoming days. All his life that habit of mind and heart stayed with him, and it is easy to imagine what a fervor of gratitude went up from his heart after the months of trial and abandonment he had gone through at the inception of the mission seminary at Steyl. The time of trial was over and the work was successfully under way at last.

But success brought, too, its needs and problems. The students and teachers had to eat and be cared for, and on him was the burden to provide. By Easter of 1876 the seminary was so crowded that the erection of additional buildings became imperative.

He said a prayer of thanks for the increase that the Blessed Trinity had brought to the work, he implored the Holy Spirit to assist him in the need of the moment, then he took up his pen and sent forth a simple statement of his need and its significance:

"The great need at present is a new building. An educational institution for fifty people requires considerable space. Therefore, in the name of God we shall build.... There is not much money available, but we know that the Lord has immense treasure houses, and our confidence will be the key to them. May we never lack this confidence! The Lord will show that He is rich enough and that no one confides in Him in vain. . . ."

The people of the neighborhood about Steyl were like most people of any given region, partly good, partly bad, partly indifferent. They had helped a great deal — the good ones; they had accepted the seminary as something outside their interest — the indifferent ones; they scanned it with malicious interest waiting its collapse — the bad ones.

This latter class thought their predictions had been fulfilled when Father Bill and Francis Reichart had left. But instead the place had seemed to obtain a new lease of life. Young boys swarmed all over it, and droves of young cassocked professors stalked sedately about it. They wondered where all the money for the whole venture came from. Eventually they found out. It came from the pockets of charity. They shook their heads when they learned that. They knew that with such a financial basis the place could not last.

On August 17, 1876, one of the men from the neighborhood, passing by, saw the ceremony of breaking ground for the new building. He hastened back to the village and spread the news around: "Now they are even beginning to build. They will certainly come to grief."

He knew whereof he spoke. Building without money is a hazardous adventure, and at the time when the building operations began, one tenth of the required sum was all that was available.

While the construction was going on, Father Janssen kept his benefactors abreast of the situation: "So far, we have been able to meet all pressing bills and we hope to be able to do so in the future. It is a strange thing to undertake to build for God. He who waits until he has the required funds in hand for a building that is necessary and intended for the glory of God and the salvation of souls will make but slow and painful progress. But he who has courage and confidence will accomplish more.... Trust in God is the virtue from which a missionary must draw all his strength and assistance. In fact a missionary must be truly heroic in his confidence in God. It is well, therefore, that our mission house, from beginning to end, be built on this virtue. All worldly and human security is absent, and yet it lacks nothing if it does not lack God. Has there ever been a monastery or ecclesiastical institution sold for debt? Never! The Lord provides for those who serve Him."

In September the funds gave out. Father Janssen's trust, however, was not unrewarded. As though by magic, benefactors appeared to pay the bills, and the structure was completed.

From this initial venture in building Father Janssen discovered a fact that was to be a guiding principle in later years.

"In erecting this first building we learned something which became very important for the development of the work. Whenever a new building was contemplated, we never asked ourselves, have we the money? But only, is the building necessary? If it was, we proceeded with courage, even though only one tenth or one twentieth of the required sum was available. We have always been able to complete the buildings and pay for them."

Some years later it was necessary to construct a church for the mission seminary. On September 8, 1884, the ninth anniversary of the founding of the seminary, the church was consecrated and Father Janssen celebrated the first Solemn High Mass in it.

He dedicated this first church of the Society to the Holy Angels. It was his firm conviction that because the Angels appeared so often as messengers of God when the redemption of the world was begun, they would also cooperate in a special manner in the gathering in of the fruits of the redemption and in the propagation of its message among the nations of the earth. He explained that as the reason for so naming the church and expressed the firm trust "that the messengers of the Faith who go forth from this institution will always experience the guidance and help of these heavenly spirits. In particular, we believe that the holy archangels, those powerful princes of heaven, will help make it certain that the petition which we so frequently direct to the hidden God of the tabernacle may be fulfilled, namely: 'May the sweet light of the Divine Word illumine the darkness of sin and paganism, and may the Heart of Jesus live in the hearts of men.'"

By leaps and bounds, in the course of the next years, buildings seemed to multiply around what had once been a simple little tavern. It was a mystery to the people of the neighborhood how this project could so expand. It was a mystery in other circles, too. The things of faith are usually a mystery to others, even to those who sometimes profess they are believers. Prayer can still work wonders undreamed of by material minded men. A work of God grows as His Providence decrees and in the manner and by the men and means

152

He has designed, and oftentimes He uses the lowliest instruments. The phenomenal growth of the seminary at Steyl was a work of God, and in achieving it He used a very prosaic little instrument of wheels and springs and bolts — a hand-operated printing press.

Chapter 17

$\mathcal{D}$URING the first days at Steyl the handling of Father Janssen's little magazine had been something of a problem. Each month the entire household journeyed to the neighboring town, unloaded the magazines from the train, hauled them to a rented room, addressed and wrapped them, hauled them off to the post office and then journeyed back to Steyl. It was a laborious arrangement, and it must have been things of this sort which brought on the criticisms of the quicker-moving and more decisive Father Bill. But the slow-moving Father Janssen was not in the least slow-thinking. His early youth on the farm had given him a love of work, but not merely of work for itself. There were just so many hours in the day, and he had seen, from his father's example, how one had to direct one's energy, organize one's effort if a livelihood was to be gotten from the stubborn soil. Work was a means, and the work of one man pitifully small and circumscribed.

154

More than one method suggested itself to him for facilitating the problem of handling his magazine. The simplest would have been to have paid someone in Paderborn to do it from there. He could also have engaged a man to handle the whole chore at Kaldenkirchen. There were other possibilities, too, but a completely different and wider view of the matter had come to him. He delayed presenting it to the others, not merely because it was as yet a totally new approach to the problem, but because, as usual, he had to refer it first to God and discover if this were what He desired. In the meanwhile they kept shipping the magazine from Kaldenkirchen.

One morning Father Janssen summoned Brother Juniper to his room. He seemed enthused about something. "Listen, Brother," he confided, "I have something to tell you. This morning, during Mass, a thought came to me, or rather, it was like a voice in my heart saying: 'Start a printing press. It will be a sword for you. You can defend the Church of God with it.'" He paused, his eyes shining bright with his plan, expectant of his brother's wholehearted agreement to this wondrous idea. Above the thicket of beard Brother Juniper's eyes looked back at him with no enthusiasm. "What do you think of the idea, Brother?" he persisted.

Thoughtfully, Brother Juniper stroked his beard. "Well," he finally announced in a grave voice, "it sounds good, I agree, but we have no one who knows anything about printing. You would have to hire a trained man. That would cost money. And then what would people outside say about this. You know what they are saying about you now. The world outside jeers at you and your work."

155

"The world! The world! I wanted to hear *your* opinion." He was disappointed that so materialistic a viewpoint should be used as a gauge for a project that had to do with God's work, even though that project had a very material aspect to it. "Well, go back to your work."

He knew what the world thought of him. That did not matter in the least to him. He had another standard, and the opinion of the world had no part in it. But the judgment of religious men did. Despite Brother Juniper's sunny disposition he had a practical head on his shoulders and a devout, truly religious heart inside his hard-working body. None knew that better than Arnold. And that was why he had first broached the matter to him. He was disappointed. He had not gotten Brother Juniper's reaction, but the world's.

It seems not to have crossed his mind that he had proposed, out of the blue, a very daring plan, and that Brother Juniper was entitled to show a corresponding caution. There was no similar enterprise that the Brother could refer to. No religious community that he knew of was in the printing business. And printing was not just something that you decided to do, and it was done. It needed machines, it needed men who knew how to run the machines. Arnold might know something about starting a seminary; he had gone through one, he was a professional teacher. But he knew nothing about printing. And when all was said and done just what did a printing press have to do with a seminary that hoped to train priests for foreign missions?

If it was all a bit confusing to good Brother Juniper it was crystal clear to Father Janssen. He hired a capable young printer from Muenster, and the very next month the first small hand press was set in operation.

It was a new departure. It was a project so totally new and so wide open to all sorts of criticism that it should have been approached very circumspectly. Moreover that was Father Janssen's usual way of procedure, cautious, prudent, waiting the auspicious moment. This seems to have been the one exception. It was evident from the very outset that he was not going to conduct the operation of his press secretly, waiting for the reaction of the world to this unheard-of activity in a religious house. He held a public dedication of the hand press, and half the village turned out to witness the event.

Father Janssen stood up before all of them and made a short speech. "We celebrate today the Feast of St. Chrysostom. His name means 'Golden-Tongued.' From his mouth there came forth words that were, for the souls of men, nuggets of gold. May the printing press of the mission seminary, also, become such a 'golden tongue' for the salvation of souls. May its products be an antidote against the poison spread by the bad press; may the publications, which shall come from this press, prove to be, for the souls of its readers, nuggets of gold. May the work of all who shall labor here, be a thing of gold, of priceless value for heaven. It is for these things that we should first of all pray."

He began to pray then, in his childlike way, for all publications that would come forth from this press, for all the readers, all the workers, and all the benefactors who had made the press possible. At last came the blessing.

157

Then Father Janssen turned the fly-wheel and the first copy of the *Little Messenger* came forth. Everyone present then took a turn at the wheel, and each took away with him, as a souvenir of the occasion, the sheet which he had printed.

It was just five months after the founding of the little mission seminary, and the struggling enterprise had used up a goodly amount of its meager funds to purchase and put in operation a printing press. The news of this extraordinary undertaking might well be considered by people outside as a rash and senseless waste of funds, and prove a deterrent to further help from benefactors. It should have been the part of human discretion to be silent about this matter, until it was evident how the project would turn out. That view of the matter never seems to have entered Father Janssen's mind.

Joyfully he published the news about this new venture, pointing out the practicality, from both spiritual and material viewpoints, for this daring innovation:

"In our days the press is a great power. It can be compared to a sword, which is wielded in the spiritual battle. A good press is a good sword unsheathed to defend the cause of God.

"Using the printing press of someone else is like using a borrowed sword, which is loaned for a few days or a few combats; but having one's own press provides one with a ready sword, always at hand and prepared for service.

"But some may ask whether the possession of a printing plant is not foreign to the spirit of a mission seminary? It is true that it was somewhat hard to make up our mind to establish our own press at this early

158

date. How many difficulties must be met by every new enterprise! Besides, everybody has a natural fear of new burdens, worry and work. But a consideration of the real character of our mission seminary helped to decide the matter.

"Our Divine Savior when enjoining upon the apostles the conversion of the world, put upon them the preaching of the word, saying, 'Preach the gospel to every creature.' In His time the printed word was unknown, but now it is known, and it is used by the devil to do much harm. Therefore, the servant of Christ must use it to do good. The printed word is a power, and the presses of a country multiply, in a single hour, the printed word a thousandfold! But it is not the mere turning out of quantities of printed matter that matters. What does matter is that the printed word be good, that it be read and taken to heart.

"In other mission seminaries one finds practical opportunities to acquire skill in various trades. How helpful this knowledge can be to the missionary! In many districts the natives expect advice from him about almost everything. A good missionary will try to do all that he can to assist them and their needs, for he knows that his skill will open to him many homes and hearts.

"This is true, also, of the press. It can be readily understood that every missionary society must provide catechisms, prayer books, and similar publications for the people of the country in which it labors. How can this be done, if none of the missionaries knows anything about printing? What they are to practice there, must be learned here.

"Since the holy archangel Michael is the patron of our seminary, we place our mission press under his

159

protection. By his humility he conquered Lucifer, and so has become the standard-bearer of the glorious, yet humble banner of the cross of Christ. May this new printing press, under his protection, assist in breaking the pride of Christ's enemies, by the humility of Christ's cross. May the principles of the saints who followed Christ, in humility and patience, guide it. These principles are far from being recognized everywhere. To uphold them will mean conflict, but, it will also mean victory. . . ."

Many a time in the months that followed Father Janssen could be seen working like a common apprentice at the press. Manfully he would crank away at the fly-wheel while the printer fed paper into the machine. Sweat, drudgery, the actual work of printing the magazine were added to the labor of writing it. But for him it was a sword, his own sword, and, small and insignificant though it was, he would keep it bright and shiny, wielding it for the sake of the King whom he loved.

After four years the *Little Messenger* had a circulation of 10,000, and an additional magazine, a weekly, was started. It was called *City of God* and was intended as a family paper. From the outset it was very popular. Eventually it became a monthly and had the largest circulation of any European Catholic magazine — three hundred and fifty thousand.

A third publication appeared a few years later: *St. Michael's Almanac.* Its circulation surpassed that of both the other publications.

A Dutch magazine, *Catholic Missions,* was the next venture. Then a child's magazine, *The Boy Jesus;* then a weekly illustrated *Weekly Post,* and finally *The Catholic Yearbook.*

160

The good that resulted from this apostolate of the press was incalculable. It brought the warmth and reality of the faith into Christian homes. It provided families with wholesome entertainment and information, as well as intellectual enjoyment. It spread the missionary spirit. To a large extent, the magazines and booklets that came from the press at Steyl were responsible for awakening interest in foreign missions throughout Germany, Austria and Switzerland. So slight had been the interest of those countries in foreign missions that, for years, the little seminary at Steyl was to have a hard struggle to exist. The establishment of the printing press was the means that saved it from extinction. It made known the needs of the new seminary and won friends and benefactors to support it. And it did much more than that. Many of its readers joined the Society.

By subscription and donation, the magazine made it financially possible to carry on the work in the foreign missions. They were a link between the missionaries in the field and the faithful at home. The articles and letters which the missionaries wrote brought home to the readers the great truth that the work of the first apostles was still being carried on, and that it was the part of all Christians to be sharers in that work, by prayer and sacrifice, by material means and spiritual.

As the years went by the apostolate of the printed word flowered into a huge enterprise. It became an integral and outstanding activity of the seminary at Steyl. The power of the press had been enlisted in the great cause of fulfilling the desires of Christ's Heart. The little sword to defend the cause of God and His Church had become a mighty weapon, that would deal telling and ever more effective blows as the years went by.

And yet it was to remain just what Father Janssen had intended it to be — a secondary, a subsidiary activity. It was integrated with the primary purpose, and rounded out more fully the lives and activities of his followers. They were working in a modern age, with modern means, for modern people. To devote oneself to the foreign missions, and forget those at home, would be a one-sided apostolate. What did it avail to bring the light to the distant darkness, and allow the light at home to die out? It was the completeness of wisdom to enlist the zeal and prayer and sacrifice of the ones at home to participate in the work of spreading the faith, and by so doing, deepen their own. And for this end the press was the modern means ready to hand.

He had able assistants in the work. His own brother, John Janssen, a spiritual writer of considerable note, was of great help; and even more so was the capable editor, Father Abel. But this project was too important for the Society as a whole, and too dear to him personally, for him to entirely relinquish its direction to others. For many years he himself managed the entire press.

This attitude of his toward the Mission Press, and his own personal share of hard and unremitting work in carrying it out had a special significance. The evangelization of a pagan country is an enterprise that carries heavy financial burdens. Father Janssen made no effort to form a missionary aid society to relieve that financial burden. He realized the value of such an organization, but he wanted to inculcate a principle, to create an attitude of mind in those who would work with him, and those who would come after. He wanted his group of men to earn its own support, as far as possible, by work. His spiritual sons were to live by the work of their hands and to eat their bread in the sweat of their brow. For the world at large, and for the people of pagan lands in particular, they were to create a new set of values, working laboriously as any man, but giving to work a new meaning, something far removed and above personal success or advancement. With their own two hands his followers were to develop the work of the missions, and by the intention that activated their labors, turn the penalty of work into a blessing for themselves and others. He wanted his followers to be animated with the same spirit of indefatigable work that animated him; and the apostolate of the press that he started so simply, so poorly, and yet so openly, was his own personal contribution as to how they, too, should face up to the reality of their needs, and by prayer and hard work overcome them.

Chapter 18

IN THE summer of 1877, Father Janssen received a letter from Archbishop Melchers of Cologne. He received many letters these days, from all strata of society, but this letter evoked strange memories. It was not so long ago that Father Janssen had sat in this prelate's office, a suppliant, asking approbation for his projected mission seminary. The reply he had received had almost ended his hopes: "We are living in a time when everything is threatening to collapse; and now you wish to build up something new!"

Those words had been spoken to him by a man suffering from the rigors of imprisonment and harassed with innumerable cares. A little more than a year ago those words had been spoken, and yet now, in the preoccupation of this busy new world of achievement in which he was living, they seemed like the echoes of a remote event, like the memory of something which had happened a very long time ago. The gathering of funds for the new building, the burden of the seminary's

164

direction absorbed him. But the letter from the Archbishop carried a plea, a request for help, a project that concerned souls, and at once all his other work was put aside.

The priests of the Archdiocese of Cologne had been unable, for three years, to make their annual retreat. Some of them were in exile, along with their Archbishop, and if ever they needed the deepening and freshening of spirit that a retreat brings, it was in these days of trial and persecution. The Archbishop had asked in his letter if Father Janssen would consider making his seminary available for his priests' retreat.

Despite the accusation of impracticalness that so many of his acquaintances had levelled against him, Father Janssen had a very sharp eye for the practical aspect of any matter. He realized at once that the holding of a retreat for priests carried possibilities of great help for his seminary. It would bring the notice of his work to many priests, enlist their aid and friendship. On the other hand, he also saw that it would entail a great many inconveniences. Accommodations were sadly lacking for even the members of the Seminary, and to house and feed additional groups, even though for a comparatively brief period, would put a burden upon all of the members of the institution.

He was aware of these practical considerations, but they seemed not to weigh much in his actual decision. What counted with him was that there was a need, a real and urgent need, that concerned not only the spiritual life of a number of priests but also of all the people in their charge. The words of his father about the value of a priest had never left his memory. A good priest was an invaluable asset to a parish. As a boy, during the Ember Days, he had prayed for good priests. He had it in his power now to contribute in a tangible way to that much desired goal. He agreed to the Archbishop's request.

On September 10, 1877, the first group of retreatants arrived. Just two days before that, on the second anniversary of the seminary's founding, the new building had been dedicated. All the priests and students had been expectantly waiting to move into the larger and more commodious quarters which the new building offered. Instead they went to work preparing the rooms for the accommodations of the retreatants. The first occupants of this new building were the priests who made the retreat. It pleased Father Janssen that the new edifice should have been first used for such a truly spiritual enterprise, and he made it a custom to inaugurate any new building by first having it used for the conducting of a retreat.

That fall one hundred and ten priests made their retreat at Steyl.

When the last of them had departed, their words of gratitude still echoing in Father Janssen's ears, the kindly deed seemed to be ended. But only apparently so. His mind had already gone from the priests who had been here, to the people for whom they cared. The priests would bring to their parishioners the good that they had garnered in the days of the retreat, but indirectly, through the example of their lives and deepened devotion. It would be so much more a direct work of help if the people themselves could make a retreat.

Up to that time, retreats for lay people in Germany had been of rather rare occurrence. In Holland the idea was entirely unknown. He decided to open the doors of the seminary to lay people for retreats. No time was lost. That very fall the first retreat was held and twenty-three men were present. It was a small beginning but the following retreats showed an amazing increase.

This new enterprise took a firm hold upon his interest. He fostered it in every way possible. With truly paternal kindness he saw to it that the retreatants were well taken care of, both as to food and accommodations. He mingled with them, spoke to them with engaging simplicity about the things dearest to his heart, the missions, and the work of his priests, the magazines. And when they were about to leave he had a rosary for each of them as a little going-away gift.

He also endeavored to foster in all the members of his Society a like friendly attitude toward the retreatants. The presence of so many outsiders entailed no small work for them. The retreats at Easter and Pentecost were always well attended, and it frequently meant that more than a thousand people had to be fed.

A year after the retreats for men were started Father Janssen was able to arrange retreats for women. He induced some of the nearby convents to provide the accommodations for the lady retreatants.

The good that resulted from the retreats was too great a joy for his heart to keep unshared. He never hesitated to tell his friends about his needs, and he never delayed in sharing with them his joys. "During September and the first part of October," he wrote, "Steyl looked almost like a place of pilgrimage. People had come, from near and far, for the purpose of spending several days in prayer and meditation upon the eternal truths. There were young men, with happy carefree countenances, serious men of middle age, and older people, some well-advanced in years; and all were animated by the one thought of learning something more of that which constitutes the great art of life — the art of dying well!

A retreat is a very important thing. Many a man has regained his peace of soul in a retreat, and many a man has been reborn by it spiritually. The memory of these days of retreat stay with one throughout life, and many a retreatant, in later life, will bless those who acquainted him with this golden opportunity."

Following the example of Steyl, very many other places in Holland, Germany and Austria were opened to crowds of retreatants. The incalculable good that resulted from all these lay retreats was the first indication for those connected with St. Michael's Mission Seminary that the secondary aims and work which Father Janssen had so steadfastly insisted be a part of the Society's program, had not been just the whim of a stubborn man, but the wise disposition of an overruling Providence.

Chapter 19

THE GREAT formative influence upon Father
Janssen's life was the intimate bonds of family life.
Not only were his ways of thought and prayer, his
private devotions, his industry and simplicity the result
of the training and example of the family circle, but
he was deeply aware of that fact. There was in him such
a deep consciousness of the influence produced by the
example of those about us, that all his ventures were
bound up with the effort to unite others into a family,
a group, working and praying for the same end. He
was attracted to the Apostleship of Prayer for that
reason, his other ventures were all efforts to group lay
people or priests together into a family with one heart
and one soul. And the tragedy of his disagreement with
his first followers had been in the complete conviction
that "unity makes strength," and despite their sincerity
there had been no unity among them.

The family was for him not only the unit of society,
it was also the exemplar of what nations and the whole

world should be: a family of nations, united in love and devotion for Christ.

Unity he wanted. How could he help but want it? From the unity of a loving family he had come, and the roots of his ideals and faith and work were sunk deep in that original source.

His own nation was travailing in a great conflict that had as its ultimate purpose the unification of the nation. But he knew that real unity did not come from external force, from compulsion, from the imposing of fines and prison sentences, from the deification of the intellect. It came from the great Oneness that was yet a Trinity. From the love of God and of God's Will, the love that could unite all men in the pursuit of one ideal, the love that did away with the fickleness of human affection and brought the great stability and permanency of the divine.

The founding day of the Society, September 8, was made into the Family Feast. A day of joy and festivity for all the members in the house, a day to bring them closer in the realization of their common aim and their common Love. For the seminary was a family — all of its members were such as "had not been born of blood, nor of the will of the flesh, nor of the will of man, but of God." But being sons of God they worked for the same end, suffered and prayed together, they failed and succeeded together, and in all their efforts they found the inspiration of mutual example, affection, and help.

The fourth Family Feast had come and gone for the little seminary in Steyl. The family had grown not only in the closeness of their common aim and purpose

170

but also in numbers. There were ten priests in the community. Five were members of the Society, five were secular priests who had temporarily identified themselves with the cause as teachers. All of these ten were not needed for professorial work. What was needed far more urgently was that the little group's flame of missionary enthusiasm find an outlet. Two of the members, Father Anzer and Father Freinademetz, never ceased urging Father Janssen to let them go to the foreign missions.

Their desires harmonized perfectly with his. He knew what the actual opening of a foreign mission could mean for the struggling little seminary. The small group at Steyl would find a constant inspiration in the fact that they were working for their own mission, that priests from their own house were fighting in the front lines for the Kingdom of God. Letters from them telling of their sacrifices, labors and successes could only arouse those in the seminary to greater loyalty and effort, deepen their own appreciation of and dedication to their vocation. And to the friends and benefactors of the seminary it would be a tangible evidence of the good their assistance was the means of accomplishing, and an inspiration for greater assistance.

But Father Janssen, if just as zealous as his ardent associates, was not as impetuous. His eyes had been turned toward China where more than four fifths of all the total number of pagans lived. To him it was the most important mission field on earth, and with his usual directness he wanted to send forth his men into the thickest of the fight, he wanted to go to the heart of the problem.

171

But none of his priests had had any missionary experience. Until he had seasoned missionaries at his command a mission field of their own was out of the question. So he wrote to Bishop Raimondi, of Hong Kong, and arranged to have him take Fathers Anzer and Freinademetz under his care and give them their initial training in actual mission work. Rome granted permission, and March 2, 1879, was set as the day of departure.

For the young mission seminary at Steyl, and especially for its founder, the day when their first messengers of the faith received the mission cross was a never to be forgotten event. Msgr. Capri, apostolic internuncio at The Hague, blessed the crosses and bestowed them upon the departing missionaries. Father Arnold Janssen preached the sermon, using the same text as he had for the opening of the seminary, three and one half years ago: "The harvest indeed is great, but the laborers are few."

"How many things have happened since the opening of this seminary! How many sufferings; but also, how many more blessings and favors of the Most High! How this house has grown, internally and externally! If today I cast a glance at the past, I do it to thank the Holy and Triune God, who has thus graciously looked down upon our weak but fruitful efforts."

He spoke then of the great land of China with its teeming millions of pagans and handful of Christians, and the obligation that was upon all of them to work for its conversion. And he turned to the two priests, Father Anzer and Father Freinademetz, who were to go forth and be the first from his small seminary to face up to the immensity of this task: "I congratulate you on this day for which you have yearned so long. It is true that it brings for you and us the sad hour of separation: you will meet on your way to the boat the tearful eyes of many loved ones, and your own hearts will sadden; but you have learned to conquer the promptings of nature, and besides you know the words of the Savior: 'He who loves father or mother more than me is not worthy of me!'

"You are going to China. You do not know what work is in store for you, nor do you know whether the Lord will bless it or not. I think you are humble enough not to take it for granted that you are destined to play a great part. You do not want to be more than others. You do not even know whether you will really reach the land of your longings. But one thing you do know — that God never leaves one's good-will unrewarded. So, go forth and face the unknown future, calmly and confidently. You will walk at the side of a loving God, and our prayers will accompany you. May the Sacred Heart of Jesus bless you, and give you a truly apostolic heart like unto His own."

After the reception of the mission cross, the two missionaries entered a waiting carriage, and Father Janssen accompanied his first two messengers of the faith to Kaldenkirchen where they boarded a train for the south. They traveled via Rome, received the blessing of the Holy Father, and on March 15 boarded a ship at Ancona. On April 20 they reached Hong Kong.

Bishop Raimondi received the young missionaries very cordially, and provided the means for their induction into all aspects of missionary work in China. He followed their progress with an interested eye, and when he wrote Father Janssen he had only words of praise

173

for the apostolic spirit that animated these two priests. Their zeal was to set a pattern, an example for the others who soon were to join them.

In 1882 South Shantung was assigned as a field of labor to the missionaries from Steyl. Father Anzer was appointed superior, and in January of that year he began active work in the town of Puoli. There were one hundred and fifty-eight Christians in the town and over twelve million pagans in the district.

Father Anzer was a man of action and a great organizer. His associates soon found that their superior's love of work was contagious, and the force of their combined efforts speedily produced results. After a year, he was able to report to Steyl: "We have baptized 1,116 pagan children in danger of death, and 687 pagans are being instructed in the Christian religion." Three years later, the mission had eight missionaries, three thousand neophytes and catechumens, one seminary, three chapels, twenty-six prayer-houses, three schools; and three thousand childen in danger of death had been baptized.

It was a promising beginning, and other successes followed. But these successes were not had without much suffering and sacrifice. The accounts of the trials and persecutions that his missionaries had to go through made hard reading for Father Janssen. He loved all of them with a deep and true affection, and their problems and sufferings were shared by him.

In May 1883, Father Anzer was assaulted and beaten into insensibility by some pagans in the town of Tscowchowfu.

In 1886, a general persecution broke out. A date was set by the enemies of Christianity for the murder of all missionaries. The men informed Father Janssen of their danger but remained at their posts. To avert the peril, Father Janssen held processions at the mission seminary at Steyl, and stormed heaven with prayer. The day set arrived and passed, and the missionaries were not molested.

Less fortunate was the outcome of the persecution by a secret society known as the "Society of the Great Knife." For three years this group waged bitter battle against everything the missionaries put their hand to. Five churches and twenty prayer-houses of the mission were reduced to ruins, and several missionaries were seriously maltreated. The heaviest blow of all was the murder of the two splendid young missionaries, Francis Nies and Richard Henle, on the night of All Saints' Day, 1897.

The German Government reacted quickly to this outrage on their nationals. They occupied Kiaochow, punished the guilty parties, and had three churches built by the Chinese Government as reparation.

Through all these events Father Janssen stood by the side of his distant missionaries. In numerous letters, full of fatherly kindness, he comforted and encouraged them. He prayed for them. In all their labors, sufferings and successes he had a part.

They were members of his own household, the first group that had gone forth from the closely knit family circle at Steyl to form another family, another household, in the midst of paganism, and by their work and prayer, bring light to the darkness.

They were far away, but in his thoughts and prayer they were very near. His one prevailing care was that the religious spirit of his missionaries might not wane.

175

He made inquiries about their keeping of the rule, their meditation, their retreats; he offered advice and suggestions to the superiors about these matters.

He was solicitous about the health of the missionaries. One of his first cares was to purchase a suitable piece of property and have it fitted up as a central house for the mission. Here all the missionaries could assemble each year, for one month, to make their retreat, hold conferences, and renew themselves physically and spiritually.

He had an eye to their practical needs, but always he was more concerned with the spiritual side of the individual. The motto that was the crusading cry for his missioners he wanted to deepen and grow in them. "May the heart of Jesus live in the hearts of men." They were associates of the Divine Word, sharers with Him in the great task of making the whole world one. In the depth of the family circle at Steyl that Divine Word had become for them a great, a vivid Reality, mysterious yet tangible, living upon the altar as the Eucharistic Word. Each morning, at the consecration of the Mass, that Word renews in an unbloody manner the Word's sacrifice on the Cross. And in communion that Incarnate Word of God, the Crucified Word, the Glorified Word sought to unite Himself to man with the closest intimacy, with the very oneness of life.

Throughout the day he wanted his missioners to remember that salient fact, that by the morning communion the Word had clothed the recipient with His divinity, without altering the human personality. In humility and patience, in suffering and joy he wanted them to imitate the Son of God, to think of things as He would think of them, to will only what He willed, to put all the strength of soul and body at His disposal, to be consumed in loving service for Him whenever, wherever He willed it.

And so by gradual degrees the Word would take full possession of them, transforming them into images of Himself, the Divine Word, divinizing them so that they could eventually say: "I live now no longer I, but Christ lives in me."

To have the Heart of Christ live in the hearts of men, he knew would need that Divine Heart to live first of all in the heart of the missionary. A man does not impart what he does not possess. And so despite his care for their health and well-being, despite the burden their financial support placed upon his shoulders, always his first and foremost interest was for the state of their growth Godwards. His motto was not merely a rallying cry, it was the fundamental fact about which all the work and prayer of every one was to converge. He never lost sight of that fact, and he never permitted others to lose sight of it. The men who formed the first family of his sons in foreign lands were grounded deeply in that truth by a father whose insistent care it was that they should never forget.

Chapter 20

THE ESTABLISHMENT of a printing press had brought a solution to many of the needs of the young and growing seminary. Financially, it was a great help, but it brought with it its own particular problem — manpower. It required skilled workers to run the machines; and skilled help was then, as now, expensive.

As the seminary expanded there were many other practical tasks that also required men. Brother Juniper had returned to his monastery and the Sisters of Divine Providence had taken over the care of the kitchen and the laundry. But the work in the printing shop, in the garden, and at the various trades required salaried help. The ever-increasing wages of these workers, along with the mechanics and laborers on the new building, became a severe drain on the seminary's slender resources.

Father Janssen knew that it would be a decided help if he could have a corps of lay helpers to assist the priests in their enterprise both at home and in the missions. The old orders had Lay Brothers to perform this service, but at that time he had no thought of founding a religious order. So he started to enlist the aid of laymen, who would be willing, out of love for God, to give their skill and labor for the cause of the missions.

Three such men came to Steyl, and gradually others followed. He had them all join the Third Order of St. Dominic. After some time he began to call them Brothers, and eventually introduced a habit for them to wear. It was a cassock that went just a little bit below the knees! His friends always said that Father Janssen was truly inventive when it came to devising means for self-humiliation, and this selection of a garb was a proof of it. The poor men who wore it had the appearance of a plucked fowl. One of the sturdy souls who survived the ordeal later on remarked: "It took a lot of courage to appear in public in such a uniform."

But the men who had the required courage and the humility found a permanent place in Father Janssen's heart. In his view of things characters that were too weak for mortification were unfit for God's work. He wanted men who were imbued with a spirit of work and prayer and mortification. He wanted the best. For only the best were fit for the great work of God.

As the seminary progressed and the work of the press expanded, the number of the Brothers grew until there were hundreds of them active at Steyl. They worked as printers, proofreaders, book binders, packers, clerks, traveling agents, linotypers, lithographers, draftsmen, photographers. They entered into all departments of the seminary's activities and gradually from their industry a small town arose, dedicated to the work of the missions. All the needs of the priests and students were

179

cared for by them. They were cooks, sacristans, porters, tailors, shoemakers, carpenters, sculptors, painters, mechanics, tinsmiths, bakers, millers, butchers, farmers, masons, plumbers and infirmarians.

Father Janssen gave them every possible chance to study the latest developments in their trades, and it always gave him great pleasure when he noticed progress in their endeavors. He would ask the Brothers to explain everything, down to the smallest details, about their work, the machine they handled, whatever it was they were engaged upon. It was amazing how his interest caused them to blossom forth and what finished work they turned out for him. His special favorites were the Brothers who humbly, faithfully, prayerfully did their jobs. He loved them. Their simplicity appealed to that deep simplicity that was his own outstanding trait. In the company of any of them he seemed to be at home. He always referred to them as "the good Brothers," and the few hours of recreation which he allowed himself on festive days, were always spent with the Brothers. If any one of them became sick he was at once an object for special care from Father Janssen.

It was necessity that caused Father Janssen to form a group of Lay Brothers. So many times in his life necessity appears to be the only reason for his taking up an enterprise or branching out into some new endeavor. But it was not merely necessity. Invariably, he had seen the need, and also the solution, long before things became acute, but it was not his way to rush into action until circumstances led up to the conclusion that this was what the good Lord wanted.

From his scientific studies he had early learned how the forces of nature were being harnessed by thousands of inventions and discoveries, and it had been his desire that they should be put to use in saving souls. For that reason motors and machines interested him, and for that reason he enlisted the aid of the Brothers who would run these motors and machines.

Very quickly he came to the realization that he had in the Brothers a valuable corps of auxiliary missionaries, and he looked forward to the day when he could send them out to the foreign missions to be active assistants to his missionary priests. Many he knew would have to remain at home, but even the ones at home would be employed in the direct service of the missions. They would be able to manufacture altars, doors, windows, and even complete dwellings which could be taken down and shipped to the foreign missions. They could assemble provisions, medicines, clothing, religious articles and forward them to those who were active in foreign lands.

In training them, Father Janssen made use of every opportunity to instill in them the supernatural viewpoint. First and foremost they were to be religious, even in the midst of their varied and technical occupations. He seemed well aware of the great problem confronting the modern worker, of the proneness that our feverish activity and spinning motors have to destroy a man's peace of soul. He asked them to do their work wholeheartedly but added: "Of course, it is necessary that you shall do your part to preserve that precious possession, your peace of soul, and put far from you whatever may threaten it."

Through the Lay Brothers Father Janssen gave an opportunity to hundreds of young men to take an active part in the propagation of the faith. Missionary activity

181

to be efficiently maintained required a firmly established base at home, and the skilled labor and cooperation of the Brothers in the seminary at home, to a great extent, took care of that need. And in the foreign fields of apostolic endeavor their function was of even greater value, for their industry and skill removed much of the burden from the shoulders of the priest, and left him freer for the actual task of preaching the gospel. To Father Janssen's mind they had a special place in the great apostolate of the missions, and he welcomed them and esteemed them. The whole balance of his own life was evenly distributed between the two great actualities of work and prayer, and there was a place for anyone at his side, a share for anyone in his crusade, regardless of the extent of talent or learning, so long as there was a love of work and prayer in the man's heart.

Chapter 21

$\mathcal{T}$HE SOCIETY that Father Janssen had formed was an active one. It had for its object external works, but it was rooted firmly in spiritual values and ideals. There was, he knew, age-old wisdom in the monastic way of life — *ora et labora* — work and pray. Absorption with material matters was not good if the inner spirit suffered, if the purpose behind the work became swallowed up in the bigness and multiplicity of external activities.

From year to year the work and activities of his seminary at Steyl increased with amazing rapidity. The steady influx of new members kept pace with the work, but the dimensions of the entire enterprise began to assume such proportions that he realized a more definite organization was needed to safeguard both the permanency of the work and the integrity of the members' idealism.

For nine years the community had been guided and governed by the regulations and practices which he and

13

Father Anzer had formulated. But now there were twenty-one priests in the Society, sixty-four Brothers and almost two hundred students. The simple formula of dedication would not be a bond sufficiently strong to hold together large numbers of missionaries scattered all over the world. New fields of labor, he knew would eventually be offered them, and it was the part of prudence that before accepting them there be a permanent bond of loyalty among his missionaries, a more solidly established basis of stability for the entire enterprise.

Father Anzer, after five years of work in China, had been summoned to Rome in order to settle a number of important problems concerning his mission field.

His arrival made it possible to set about the task of revising the statutes.

On December 10, 1884, Father Anzer, Father H. Wegener, who was Prefect of Studies, and Father John Janssen, gathered with Father Arnold Janssen at Steyl and opened the first General Chapter of the Society. With great care and thoroughness they went into the work of rewording and revising the statutes. For weeks and months the four men labored and prayed, debated and discussed all the internal and external activities of the Society.

When their deliberations were ended, not only had a complete constitution been formulated, but a religious congregation had emerged. The name of the Society was retained as the "Society of the Divine Word," but there was now prescribed in place of the individual member's dedication to the Society the three religious vows, both for clerics and for Lay Brothers. The details of entrance and admission to the Society, of its scope and purpose were fully and concisely formulated. The rule was clear and complete, a set of regulations on a par with those of any other religious order.

One new element had been introduced. From this time forth the special veneration of the Holy Spirit was enjoined upon all the members of the Society. Every year, seven Masses were to be said for the sanctification of those marriages from which the Holy Spirit would draw priests for the Church and for the Society.

An election was held and Arnold Janssen was chosen to be the Superior General of the Society, for life.

The deliberations of the Chapter closed on May 12, 1886.

This first formal constitution of the Society of the Divine Word was submitted to the Bishop of Roermond and received his approbation. In the years that followed other general chapters were held and their revisions of the constitution were carefully examined by the same Bishop and approved. In February, 1889, Father Janssen made a formal petition to Rome for papal approbation of the Society of the Divine Word and its constitution, and on January 25, 1901, the approbation was granted.

It had taken a matter of twenty-six years for the enterprise at Steyl to mature. Through conflict and poverty, by the prayer of the good and the sacrifices of the poor, by the opposition of the knowing and the work of the zealous, the enterprise had come to the fulness of a well-ordered religious congregation. Its beginnings had been small and poor; it had been placed like a small seed in the dark soil of an alien country-side, and there, by the side of a quiet stream, it had lain like a thing of death, unnoticed by the busy world of the day. But, in God's good time, from the death of the seed had come forth life, vigorous life, abundant life, a life that would spread its vital fruitfulness to all the ends of the earth.

Chapter 22

$\mathcal{T}$HE STORM of persecution which had been raging for several years against the Catholics of Germany at last showed signs of abating. Priests were allowed to resume work in their parishes. As a result, many of the secular priests, who had been acting as teachers in St. Michael's Mission Seminary, returned to Germany to take up pastoral work in the dioceses to which they belonged. Young priests of the Society had to take over the teaching tasks of the Seminary.

The thorough training of these priests for their important function became an immediate concern for Father Janssen.

He wanted teachers who would not only be scientifically learned but who would be also deeply imbued with the right spiritual and ecclesiastical attitude of mind. There was only one answer to this need — Rome, the center of Catholic philosophy and theology and worship.

In 1888, St. Raphael's College, the second establishment of the Society, was started in Rome. Father John Janssen was appointed rector. The little institution had

187

an even more humble beginning than the one at Steyl. It was located in a rented house in the northeastern part of the city.

The number of its residents was small: one Lay Brother to take care of the house, and from two to five clerics. The priests attended the various Roman universities — the Propaganda, Gregoriana, Apollinar, and especially the university of the Dominicans, Minerva.

It was a little house, this dwelling in Rome, but it produced great good. From it there went forth, in the course of time, a number of excellent teachers, deeply versed in Catholic thought and science, and thoroughly imbued with the principles of faith and devotion to the Holy See — qualities which they transmitted to their students. At the same time, this little institution formed a connecting link between the Society and the Holy See. In his official dealings with the Roman authorities, the rector of St. Raphael's College would represent the Society.

The heads of most religious orders maintain a residence in Rome for that very purpose, and when the question was put to Father Janssen as to why he did not do likewise, he had a very detailed reply.

"I have thought the matter over very carefully," he stated, "and considered it before God in prayer, and my conclusion is this: All our houses are in Germany and Austria. My presence is necessary there, because their direction from a distance would be rather difficult; that is one reason. A second one is that, while the Society is still so small, it would seem to savor somewhat of pretentiousness to try to appear 'big' in Rome. And you will admit that things pretentious do

188

not come from God. Modesty and reserve seem to be more indicated in our case. For that reason, I have never desired that my person or our young Society should be mentioned publicly, in an obtrusive manner, as though we were anxious to play a great part. Modesty and humility will draw the blessing of God upon our work. Ostentation and pompousness are a hindrance to the intentions of God, who chooses what is small and insignificant before the world to carry out His designs. The college of St. Raphael can handle our communications with the Roman Curia."

Through this college in Rome a constant supply of well-trained teachers for the theological and philosophical branches was assured. Other young priests were sent to German universities, to give them an opportunity for higher studies in the natural sciences, mathematics, and linguistics. At the universities of Berlin, Bonn, Innsbruck, Munich, and Vienna, they came in contact with the most prominent scholars and acquainted themselves with the methods of modern scientific procedure.

While the acquisition of scientific knowledge was the chief purpose of these special studies, Father Janssen made it plain that there was another reason underlying them. These young priests, for a number of years, had been studying and training in secluded ecclesiastical institutions. They were expected by their attendance at public universities, to establish a fresh contact with the realities of modern life and the needs and aims of the present day, learning at the same time to appreciate the accomplishments of other able men, and, through their example, to become animated with a genuine love for work and persevering diligence.

189

He knew the dangers of one-sidedness. For that reason he did not send his men to one university but to different ones. He did not prescribe what branches of study they were to pursue. That was left up to their own inclination and choice. But he did expect minute reports about everything, and thorough use of their opportunities, as well as loyalty to the Society which had given them the chance for this special training.

The great formative influence for the molding of a character was to him the family. But he knew, from personal experience, that next to it was that of the school. He had been in a number of them as a student, he had spent too extended a period of his early priesthood as a professor, not to have realized that. For that reason he expended a great deal of care and money to obtain capable teachers, for he knew that all the paraphernalia of education, classrooms, auditorium, campus and equipment are but adjuncts; the school is really the men who teach in it.

For fifteen years, despite his many other duties as rector of the seminary and manager of the magazine and director of the press and head of the entire Society, he himself taught at Steyl. Mathematics, his first love, remained his principal branch. Wherever possible, he gave his young teachers practical hints about teaching methods. Up to the last years of his life, he personally presided over the examinations, oral and written, which lasted for several days.

He spared no pains to bring the Society's curriculum up to the highest scholastic level. Prominent specialists in this line were consulted to have the benefit of their views and experience. It was too important a matter, he felt, for any half measures.

190

The details of the teaching work in the Society — the textbooks, the methods of teaching; the ways and means used to advance and further the various studies — these were matters of abiding solicitude for him all his life. In one of the frequent conferences he gave to his teachers he disclosed his vigorous views of what was to him one of the Society's main instruments for accomplishing its aims.

"One of the chief activities in the missions is teaching. That has been proved in the past. Those who have received a higher education are destined to have a decisive influence over their contemporaries; for that reason it is essential that they be instructed and trained in the religious spirit. Today this is even more necessary than formerly, because unbelief is more and more taking possession of the schools. If nothing is done to counteract this, everything will eventually be lost."

With the greatest care he saw to it that all the educational and scientific endeavors of his priests should be imbued with the spirit of faithful adherence to the mind of the Church. *"Sentire cum ecclesia"* (To think with the Church) was to him a guiding star and a pledge of blessing and success in teaching. To deviate from this rule he considered disastrous. On one occasion he commented on the sad effects which the rationalistic *Zeitgeist* was having upon the sacred sciences.

"The days are bound to be sad for Holy Church," he declared, "when people come to think that every tradition, because it is old, must be abolished, when everybody wishes to offer something new, when teachings prevail that have been invented and constructed by mere vanity and conceit. Such teachers, instead of submitting humbly to authority, try to mold and change

191

the word of God according to their own whims. But it is self-will and stupidity they offer, and not genuine gold. Therefore it fails to endure. How differently did the great St. Thomas think and act. He appreciated everything good in the past and gladly built on the foundations of others. How often does he refer to other authorities: *'Ut Augustinus dicit; ut Magister dicit.'* "

His solicitude to preserve among the teachers of the Society the spirit of fidelity to the faith was manifested time and again.

"If religious communities wish to have the blessing of God upon the labors, they must strive above all to take a vigorous stand in the defense of pure Catholic doctrine. They must never fraternize with the spirit of modern times which tries to apply the idea of liberty to the realm of religion in such a way that great harm is done to souls."

Whenever he observed that scientific efforts were being made in the right spirit, he encouraged them in every possible manner. He would show unusual interest, listen for hours to reports on the work done, ask many questions, and give plain sound advice on an amazing variety of subjects.

In his letters to the missionaries he directed them to gather and send to Europe any material that would be of value for research work in anthropology, geology, and linguistics. Though always economical and insisting on the spirit of poverty, he gladly granted money for scientific purposes, apparatus, books and magazines.

One of his priests, Father William Schmidt, under Father Janssen's guidance was led into the paths of learning that have made his name world-famous. He founded an international anthropological and ethnological review, *Anthropos;* wrote some one hundred and fifty books, became a member of the Papal Academy of Science, a Laureate of the French Academy and a Doctor *Honoris Causa* of over a dozen famous universities.

Yet to the amazement of all, this man, who is pre-eminently a scientist, is known throughout several countries as a preacher and director of retreats and as a composer of church music. But to those who knew of his formation at the hands of Father Janssen, there is no cause for wonder. He is but the ripe fruit of a great teacher's teaching. He has but carried out in his life the instruction so solicitously imparted by a man who was not only a capable teacher but a loving father, and who wrote to him on the occasion of the *Anthropos'* first appearance:

"I congratulate you on the success that your magazine has had so far. You have done everything in your power for its success. You have worked hard. I know that you will not lose sight of your supernatural aim. Working for God will bring you His blessing. At the same time you will realize that it is not going to be easy to keep an undertaking of this kind going, after the novelty of it has worn off. That is why the blessing from above is all important.

"Let us often remind ourselves, therefore, that we work for the greater glory of God and His Church, for Catholic science, for the good of the Society, and especially for the good of the enemies of the Church, that they may know that Catholic missionaries do not disdain but rather cherish and further science, as far as we are able."

193

Chapter 23

I T HAD always been Father Janssen's intention that his mission seminary was to be not only for Germany and Holland but also for Austria-Hungary. As the years went by, and building after building was being added to St. Michael's Mission Seminary at Steyl, it became manifest that before long a branch institution would have to be opened. His mind kept turning to Austria as the logical location. After mature deliberation and prayer, he journeyed to Austria and obtained an interview with the Archbishop of Salzburg. He had no intentions of obtaining definite results from this interview, but wanted to lay his plans, as usual, before one in authority to discover the reaction, to find guidance as to whether his project should be undertaken or discarded.

He came into the presence of the Archbishop with no recommendations from anyone, without even an introduction. Briefly he outlined his plan, and then awaited the Archbishop's comments.

"You have in mind the founding of a mission seminary here in Austria," said the Archbishop. "That I

194

gather, Father, is the gist of what you have told me. Is it not?"

"Yes, your Grace."

"How much money have you collected so far toward that enterprise?"

"Nothing, your Grace. Not a penny."

The Archbishop stared at him. "To found a seminary you need money — a great deal of money. You must be aware of that."

"I am, your Grace," he replied simply.

"Without money you cannot do what you propose."

"God will provide when the hour has come," replied Father Janssen confidently.

The Archbishop looked into those candid eyes and saw there the absolute confidence that can come from only one source. It was not his custom to encourage projects that started out with nothing but confidence, but the eyes of Father Janssen held more than empty self-confidence. He recommended him to a priest in Vienna who would assist him in his undertaking.

Eight times Father Janssen journeyed to Austria on this matter. On May 7, 1883, he had his first audience with Emperor Francis Joseph. The Emperor listened to his petition with visible interest and graciously accepted the document in which the entire project was more fully explained. The matter was then turned over to the minister of education.

Endless negotiations ensued. According to the existing laws Father Janssen had to be a qualified teacher and also an Austrian citizen. He was a qualified teacher. There was no difficulty on that score. But in order to assume Austrian citizenship a number of formalities had to be gone through before he was allowed to take his oath of allegiance in the presence of the Austro-Hungarian Ambassador in The Hague, Holland.

These preliminary requirements having been met, he submitted the copy of the curriculum which the new seminary intended to follow. It aroused immediate and strong opposition. He was asked to adapt his plan of studies to the regulations of the State, and to place the institution under State supervision. He could not accede to these demands. The purposes of his Society he explained, patiently and at length, demanded an entirely different curriculum, and the internal independence of the seminary had to be preserved at any cost. It was very hard to convince the authorities of this necessity. Many an hour he waited in the ante chambers of state officials, many a time he was rebuffed, more than once he was subjected to the petty meanness and irritating hauteur of officialdom. But that seemed to matter little to him. The great aim he had in view was the only thing that mattered. His spirit of sacrifice was as long-lasting as his perseverance, and his efforts met with eventual and complete success.

On October 14, 1888, the document authorizing the opening of the seminary was signed by the Emperor. It had taken seven years of work and weary waiting to obtain that important document.

He had set his heart on locating the new seminary near the capital of the Empire. Vienna had a great dearth of priests, and Father Janssen hoped that his spiritual sons might, to some small extent, be of help in rebuilding the religious life of that region. Moreover, the proximity of a large university and the many scientific advantages which the museums and libraries

196

of the capital offered were a practical inducement that he could not disregard.

A suitable piece of property at Moedling, about twelve miles South of Vienna, was purchased.

The new mission seminary was named in honor of the archangel St. Gabriel. In the very first statutes he had drawn up for his Society he had named the three archangels as patrons. The seminary at Steyl had been dedicated to the archangel St. Michael; the institute at Rome was named after St. Raphael; the establishment in Austria was named after St. Gabriel. On April 26, 1889, the cornerstone of St. Gabriel's Mission Seminary was laid. Father Janssen accompanied the three strokes of the hammer with the following words: "For the greater glory of the Holy Ghost, the God of eternal love!

"For the welfare of our Holy Mother, the Catholic Church, and for the spreading of her salvation and her blessings over the nations who do not yet know her!

"For the spiritual good of this region and this empire!

"Under the protection of the holy archangel St. Gabriel, and all the holy patrons of the Society of the Divine Word!"

The new institution was intended not only for higher studies, but also as a focal point for the special veneration of the Holy Ghost. His brother, Father John Janssen, whose love and zeal for the Holy Spirit were truly inspiring, was made Rector of the new seminary. It was through his efforts that a large and splendid church in honor of the Holy Ghost was eventually erected at St. Gabriel.

Emperor Francis Joseph paid a visit to the seminary on October 3, 1894, and this sign of imperial favor brought a great deal of favorable attention and assistance to the new venture.

197

Father Janssen made it a custom to spend several weeks each year at St. Gabriels. It was not just to give the retreat for those who were to be ordained, to prepare them by numerous conferences and practical instructions for their priestly activity, but to discharge the onerous task of assigning to the newly ordained their future field of labor. He labored carefully, prayerfully, meticulously over that important task. He realized that a mistake here could not be easily rectified.

If a Bishop makes an unsuitable appointment for a young priest he can easily enough adjust it by transferring the priest to some other part of the diocese. But it was a different matter in his Society, when the choice was between China or Europe, between educational or administrative work, pastoral labors or scientific pursuits. "This is no matter to be settled in haste," he assured his advisers. "We must pray and have others pray, and also reflect a great deal after we have all the necessary and best available data. What pains I take to make the right choice, going over all my memoranda again and again most carefully!"

But his visits to St. Gabriel's if bound up with much work and cares yet were always looked forward to with peculiar pleasure. The church there was very dear to him. He called it "the Sanctuary of the Holy Spirit." He found in its beauty and peacefulness something that answered deeply the aspirations of his heart. "How often has this church reminded me of the beauty of heaven! It is indeed a great grace for our Society that we have such a beautiful church dedicated to the Holy Ghost. I am convinced that He will dispense many graces to all who come here to worship in his house."

Chapter 24

*I*N THE course of the negotiations for opening a seminary in Austria Father Janssen had been obliged to go to Rome. While there he had an audience with Pope Leo XIII, and the Supreme Pontiff had asked him if he were in a position to take over one of the German colonies as a mission field. Father Janssen replied that the Pontiff's wish would be law to him. The Pope then asked if he had not thought of founding a mission seminary in Germany itself. Father Janssen explained that there was a military service law in Germany that was incumbent on all, and that he did not think the Reichstag would pass a law freeing members of religious orders from it. The Pope was of the opinion that the German Government might eventually be led to show a favorable attitude toward the project.

With much wisdom and with patient carefulness, Pope Leo worked for the bringing about of better conditions and more peaceful times in Germany. After several years the fruit of his labors began to appear with the gradual abolition of the "May laws."

One of the first evidences of it was that the German Government entered into negotiations with Father Janssen about the question of a mission seminary. Bishop Kopp of Breslau was deputed by the Government to act as its intermediary.

Pope Leo had written to the Imperial Chancellor Prince Bismarck, requesting permission to establish a mission seminary in Germany. Bismarck informed Bishop Kopp of the Government's interest, and negotiations began. Father Janssen was summoned to Berlin. Questions were asked of him about the Society, its purposes, its nature, its means of support. He answered calmly, clearly and convincingly all the queries that were put to him. The historical importance of the event in which he was playing so important a role seems in no way to have ruffled him. Months and years of negotiations followed but he walked quietly through it all.

Very prudently he inquired and put questions, and very carefully he studied all aspects of the matter. He was so frank in all his replies and dealings that it compelled even the devious officials to meet his frankness with frankness. The colonial director frankly admitted to him that the Government had absolute need of the missionaries. "Without missionaries," he explained, "there is no civilization; and without civilization our colonies are of no value." He assured Father Janssen that the Government would not meddle with the religious activity of the missionaries, and said that he wanted to have the Divine Word missionaries take charge of the colony in Togo.

Interviews with government ministers and officials succeeded one another. Eventually Father Janssen learned that the Government intended to admit only one religious congregation to its colonies and that this would be the Society of the Divine Word. Father Janssen was to have control over all the missionary activity in the German colonies and the exclusive right to establish mission seminaries in Germany. Bishop Kopp urged him to act at once and ask the Government for permission to open several missionary seminaries.

It was a most alluring prospect, a gigantic field of labor, and there would be at his command every means to cultivate it. The months and years of meetings and deliberation had drawn out wearingly long, and now suddenly success was in his hand. But it did not move him into hasty action. He moved with even greater quiet and reserve.

In the alluring plan he saw many doubtful features, and foremost among them there was the grave danger that his work would be characterized as a "Royal-Prussian" missionary society.

The Minister of Religious Affairs became irked by his delay to close with the Government's proposal. He offered him several sites for his first missionary seminary, and in order to exert pressure on him told him that he had better make a quick decision, because the Fathers of the Holy Ghost were desirous of opening a seminary in Prussia, and they had the recommendation of the Archbishop of Cologne. Father Janssen's reply was immediate: "I beg your Excellency to allow the Fathers of the Holy Ghost to come in, and that you will give them permission to found a house. I shall gladly stand back."

The Minister was greatly surprised. He had intended to exert pressure upon Father Janssen and had succeeded in doing just the opposite. Nor could he manage to elicit Father Janssen's assent to the project until it was made clear that other religious orders also would be allowed to found houses in Germany. He then agreed to open a seminary in Silesia.

Property in that province was purchased, but before the cornerstone was laid a storm of opposition broke loose. It was claimed that the new mission seminary would exploit the goodhearted people of Silesia and would take away the needed candidates for the priesthood from the diocese of Breslau. The opposition was definitely a very vocal one and at times even violent, and it spread into the highest circles of the Church.

Father Janssen did not desire a public defense against these unjust attacks. To the editor of the Catholic paper which headed the opposition, he wrote: "Despite your provocation I shall not send anything for publication in your paper. I do not like to correspond about such things in a manner which tends to excite only wonderment among Catholics and secret joy among our adversaries. I ask you most earnestly to desist from the publication of these ill-advised articles. The time will come when our contemplated mission seminary will, despite all present opposition, carry out its proper share and type of activity; and the remembrance that your paper published these articles will then not be a pleasant one for you."

A publisher by the name of Francis Niese wrote to Father Janssen to tell him that he had obtained the permission of Bishop Kopp to defend him: "Our task," he explained, "is to prepare the way for your work. It does not matter that a few hard words, more or less, are exchanged. I am not at all surprised at what is happening. History proves that it was always thus. Such things are as necessary as the cross on the altar. I need not tell you that I am heart and soul in favor of your work."

Father Janssen begged Mr. Niese to refrain from making a public defense of him and his work, but Mr. Niese was too much interested in the cause of the seminary to heed this advice. A particularly pointed article by him had immediate results. The opposition at once ceased, at least insofar as the public press was concerned.

Unfortunately, the turmoil aroused by the opposition had an effect upon the Government. They delayed their final approbation of the seminary in Silesia until matters had completely quieted down.

Very fittingly Father Janssen gave to this new seminary the name of "Holy Cross." He had had much trouble with its founding, but in later years much joy was to come to him from the growth and development of this institution.

When the Holy Cross Mission Seminary was finally and fully established, Father Janssen turned his eyes toward the western part of Germany. St. Michael's Mission Seminary at Steyl was no longer able to accommodate all the applications for students. A second house was necessary. He obtained an estate near St. Wendel, and on the 30th of November he dedicated the new seminary there. It was called St. Wendelin's Mission Seminary after the patron saint of that region.

The defective condition of the roads in and about the estate were the cause of much inconvenience to this new foundation. As a result, for a long time, there was always repair work being done on the old roads, and the building of new ones. Whenever Father Janssen made a trip to St. Wendelin's he would zestfully take part in these labors. He would exchange his cassock for a coat, and his shoes for high boots. Although he was past sixty now he would direct the leveling and excavating work, handling pick and shovel himself, an example and inspiration for the others.

The four flourishing seminaries of the Society made Father Janssen's name and work widely known. As a result he received many letters from priests and people concerning favorably situated properties for future establishments. He had already three houses for Germany, St. Michael's, Holy Cross and St. Wendelin's, and only one in Austria. He had always expected much from Austria toward the furtherance of the mission cause, but the one house he had in that country, St. Gabriel's, was for higher studies. He wanted a preparatory seminary.

A beautiful piece of property was obtained and the new mission seminary of St. Rupert was erected.

Within a span of thirty-three years Father Janssen had founded five missionary establishments. The development of his Society had been so rapid that it would have been easy for him to open a greater number of houses. But he always moved with great precaution.

When he began his work at Steyl his house was the only one of its kind in all of Germany, Austria-Hungary, Holland and Switzerland combined. Following his example there were soon, besides his own houses, nineteen mission seminaries representing various missionary congregations.

This manifestation of mission spirit was a source of deep joy for him. He had experienced, in the founding of Holy Cross, narrow-mindedness from others, but he had not answered like with like, for there was in him a truly apostolic broad-mindedness. When other communities entered into the field of work with him he was genuinely pleased and happy. There was no attitude of fear or of enviousness. How could there be? The advance of Christ's Kingdom in the hearts of men required countless apostles; his Society alone could not accomplish it. It was only one small division in an army that must take in all the world till not only every individual, but all families and nations were won to Christ. The presence of other communities might lessen the numbers of applicants for his own work. That made no difference. It was not essential that his Society should outstrip others in the numbers of applicants and members. The essential thing was: "that in every way ... Christ is being proclaimed; in this I rejoice, yes and I shall rejoice" (Phil. 1-18).

Chapter 25

THE FIRST mission the Society of the Divine Word had taken over was in China. Its second mission was the little German colony of Togo on the west coast of Africa. On the map it was merely an insignificant spot, but in reality it contained about a million inhabitants.

Portable tropical houses had been constructed at Steyl and shipped by sea to this mission district. The Brothers reassembled them there, and the missionaries had quick and adequate housing. And this was a long time before our era of pre-fabricated dwellings.

At the end of the first year three stations had been opened, but the rigors of tropical climate soon claimed some victims. Five of the missionaries succumbed to fever.

The climatic difficulties, the hostility of the fetish worshipers, the moral degradation of the adult Negroes — these were the things which made mission life in Togo a real sacrifice.

And yet in spite of difficulties the mission progressed

splendidly. Particular attention was paid to the construction of schools, and before long Togo had more schools than any other West African mission district.

The next mission entrusted to the Society of the Divine Word was New Guinea. The first band to go there was composed of three Fathers and two Brothers. As with any prospective mission field, Father Janssen had tried to gather exact information about this new field of labor. All the books available on the subject were studied, oftentimes into the late hours of the night. There were many serious obstacles to New Guinea's evangelization. Morally and culturally, the Papuans were on a very low level. Witchcraft and infanticide prevailed everywhere. No fewer than three hundred languages were spoken in the coastal villages.

What particularly interested Father Janssen in this field of labor was the missionaries' attempt from the outset to make this mission self-supporting. They transplanted cattle and horses; they started up plantations and farms, they trained the natives to become industrious and self-supporting. A steam sawmill was installed at the chief station. The lumber from this mill was used for the construction of the mission stations as well as for government trading posts.

A small steamer was purchased for maintaining communications between the mission stations along the five hundred miles of coastline. It was under the command of Brother Canisius, who held a captain's license.

The astounding progress of modern Japan announced the coming of a new era for the Far East. Father Janssen was well aware of that and when an opportunity presented itself for sending missionaries to this country, he eagerly seized it. Six districts from the

207

diocese of Hakodate and the archdiocese of Tokyo initiated the work of the Society there.

The last mission field which Father Janssen took over was the Philippines. The province of Abra was assigned to the Society of the Divine Word.

Besides these strictly foreign missions, he had had his men active for a number of years in South America, notably in Argentina, Ecuador, Brazil and Chile.

One would have thought that with his instinct for the important, the vital, he would have founded a seminary, at a very early date, in the United States. It was a progressive nation, its size, resources and population immense, and the Church had advanced proportionately with the nation.

But it was not his way to take the initiative. He waited until external circumstances indicated a new venture, and most of the missions and works he had assumed had been the result of a direct approach from someone outside.

His approach to the United States was a very prosaic one. The Father in charge of the press was very much aware of the large numbers of German-speaking people in that country and wished to increase the number of subscribers to the magazines. A Brother was sent to the United States to canvass.

From that lowly start there developed the work of the Divine Word Fathers in the United States.

The first permanent settlement was made on a farm outside of Chicago near the present town of Northbrook. It started out as an industrial school for boys, but later on developed by various stages into St. Mary's Mission Seminary, the Society's largest and most flourishing enterprise in this country.

It began in poverty and hardship, a poverty comparable to the original beginning at Steyl. It took years before it developed into an institution of any importance. But the slowness of its development would not have bothered Father Janssen. "I do not like mushrooms," he was wont to say, "that shoot up during the night. I like good solid trees that take time for their growth, and grow firm roots." The American project was slow in starting but once it was under way it developed and spread soundly and well. There are now mission seminaries in seven different states, and its work among the Negroes, notably its seminary at Bay Saint Louis, Miss., which has turned out twenty-four negro priests, is outstanding.

The seed for all these projects had been small, but the growth from it had been amazingly wide and far. If Father Janssen looked on it and rejoiced, his joy held no self-complacency. He was too down to earth, too much a child of God not to see clearly the true source of the work's greatness and expansion. He had worked hard, long days that started at 4:00 a.m. and ended late at night, but for him work without the supporting spirit of faith was a body without a soul. "When you see the earth parched," he was wont to say, "and plants shriveling up and dying for lack of rain, consider: Without God's blessing and grace, all my activities can only remain sterile and unproductive." And it was with that same attitude that he viewed the astonishing increase of his Society and its work. "Let us be convinced," he said, "that most of the good accomplished so far has come as a result of God's blessing; and this blessing will increase and grow, the more we try to live according to the spirit of faith...."

209

Chapter 26

*W*HEN THE persecution in Germany was reaching its height, it seemed but a matter of a short while before all priests, Brothers and Sisters would be expelled from the country. At that time Father Janssen had written an article addressed to the Superioresses of religious sisterhoods. In it he called their attention to the grave peril that confronted them, and, at the same time, he brought forward the possibilities that opened up for them to engage in foreign mission work. He pointed out that nuns and Sisters had a special task to perform in the field of the foreign missions. It was far easier for Sisters to approach and influence the women of a pagan people than priests or Brothers. To a great extent the task of transforming pagan women into Christians was their line of work; and how important that was for the entire work of evangelization he clearly indicated. "The priestly calling is a grace of God; and only rarely does God work a miracle of grace.

210

As a rule, He allows good to grow and develop in the Church in a slow and natural way. The grace of a priestly vocation, you can observe, in nearly all the periods of history, has ripened and matured in the bosom of good Christian families. Generally priests are the offspring of pious mothers. The prayer and virtue of the mother have fostered the grace granted their sons.

"It is evident, therefore, that what the foreign missions need are many pious mothers, and it is the Sisters who, to a great extent, can bring that about."

In 1877 Bishop Daniel Comboni paid a visit to Steyl. He spoke at great length to Father Janssen about the remarkable activity of the Sisters in his mission and suggested that he should found a congregation of missionary Sisters. Father Janssen was much impressed, but, at the time, all his efforts and thought were absorbed in the task of keeping the seminary at Steyl in existence.

In 1881 a Miss Helen Stollenwork wrote and asked him to assist her in becoming a missionary Sister, but there was little he could do to help her. There were no German missionary Sisters at the time. She came to Steyl to discuss the matter with him, and the upshot of their meeting was that she decided to assist the work of the missions, for the time being, by helping the Sisters who were in charge of the kitchen. Father Janssen agreed that in the event of his founding a congregation of missionary Sisters she would be received.

Three other girls joined her. Patiently and faithfully these four women worked and prayed, over a period of several years.

The year of 1888 brought a change in their status, Brothers took over the kitchen work. The four women, along with the Sisters of Providence, had to leave. Father Janssen gave them a cottage to live in, a cottage which the students of the seminary used to call "the convent under the three linden trees." They remained there for almost a year and a half doing the mending for the seminary.

Circumstances eventually seemed to indicate to Father Janssen that the founding of a congregation of missionary Sisters was the Will of God. It was difficult to carry on modern mission activity without the aid of missionary Sisters. Their assistance was essential for conducting girls' schools, orphanages, hospitals, dispensaries and for the instruction of women in catechism. It seemed to him it would make for greater efficiency and solidarity if his missionaries worked with Sisters of a congregation allied to theirs rather than with strangers.

Added to this was his deep conviction that prayer was an all-important means for forwarding the work of the missions. The quiet life of prayer and sacrifice which the four women led, had edified him very much. He could vision what a tremendous aid a whole congregation of such praying souls would be for drawing down God's blessing upon his Society.

More than once he had been urged to proceed, but twelve years had elapsed before he was ready to undertake the new enterprise. In November, 1889, a neighboring monastery became vacant and he purchased it and designated it as the residence for those who were to become missionary Sisters. On December 7, 1889, the candidates moved in.

212

The first draft of the rules for this new community took him two years to compose. The final draft was completed in 1892 and the local Bishop approved of it the following year.

In the meantime the little community had speedily grown to more than thirty members. Sixteen of them were invested with the habit on January 17, 1892. They had a blue habit, blue scapular, and white veil. These colors were to remind the Sisters of the fundamental virtues of their calling, humility and innocence. The name given their congregation was "Sister Servants of the Holy Ghost."

The special tasks assigned them were veneration of the Holy Ghost; active sharing by work and prayer in the propagation of the faith, and special prayer for priests and for the sanctification of souls.

He devoted a great deal of his time to training the minds and hearts of the Sisters. He gave them every opportunity to prepare for the tasks that awaited them in the missions. Missionary Sisters were required to be versed in many branches of work, but above all he needed teachers for girls' schools. For that reason he arranged a three-year normal course for the ones who were to teach. But his chief aim always was to cultivate a truly religious spirit in them. Ability without piety meant nothing to him.

On September 11, 1895, Father Janssen was able to hand the mission cross to the first Sisters who were to go to foreign lands.

In his sermon he showed that the command of Christ, "Go ye into the whole world and preach the gospel to every creature" was meant for all members of the Church, and that women also, in the manner suitable

213

to them were bound to work for its realization. "How grand is your work," he said; "it is a work for which the Son of God Himself came down from heaven. It is a work that will bring the greatest rewards in heaven. Therefore, we have every reason to congratulate these missionary Sisters who today enter upon these holy tasks. Despite the sorrow and tears of parting, we can find it in our hearts to congratulate the relatives of these Sisters, who have come here to say farewell to them, probably for life. And we do congratulate them, because they have consented to the sacrifice of their daughters or sisters, and have given them to God. They will be richly rewarded for this, you may be sure, and they will share in the merits of all the good works performed by these devoted Sisters. And you, dear Sisters, have no fear; the strong hand of God will comfort you, and His holy angels will accompany you."

This first contingent was followed by others. Each succeeding year witnessed another band of missionary Sisters going forth, and the reports that came back to Father Janssen about their zeal and success was a joy to his heart.

The numbers of young women who asked for admittance rapidly increased to the point where he could go ahead with the completion of his plans for their institute. From the outset he had visioned the Sisters along the pattern of Mary and Martha, as a double congregation, one group to be devoted to active works, the other to the contemplative life.

Seven years after he had founded the Sisters Servants of the Holy Ghost he inaugurated the cloistered branch of this order. The first members were six of the missionary Sisters, who had requested permission to enter the cloistered group. For their religious garb, Father Janssen designated a rose-colored habit with white veil and white scapular. This Pentecostal color of their habit was to remind the Sisters that their special work was to revere the Holy Ghost, and to implore the coming of His divine fire upon the cold pagan world. Their occupation was prayer and handiwork. Hidden in perfect solitude they were to lead a life entirely consecrated to God, in prayer and mortification, and thus draw the grace of the Holy Ghost upon the entire Church, especially upon the priesthood, and in particular, upon the priests of the Society of the Divine Word. There was soon a sufficient number of them to have perpetual adoration. They alternated every hour before the tabernacle. To praise and adore God, to pray for all souls on earth — that was the first and most important task of these Sisters, that, according to Father Janssen, was to be their mission work.

He often spoke about this to them and endeavored to instill in them a devotion that would be wide and unselfish. "What is demanded of you," he explained, "is not that you pray for the miserable little intentions which concern yourselves. Those should be left to the kindness of God. You should pray for the big intentions of the world. St. Teresa was often asked to pray for small things, but she admonished her daughters most earnestly not to lose sight of the important intentions, the ones that concerned the glory of God and the conversion of the world. Those, too, are the intentions for which you must pray. Some day you will be judged as to whether you have fulfilled that duty faithfully."

It might appear that the nuns should pray most of all for the propagation of the faith, but Father Janssen told them they should pray first for priests, because, through the priests, Christian families would be sanctified, and vocations, both for the priesthood and the missions, increased. With that in mind he assured them: "You are the representatives of all our seminaries and of the entire Church."

The basis of all his thinking, of all his planning and activity was rooted in the firm conviction that without the grace of God nothing can be accomplished. And grace could be obtained by prayer. His founding of a congregation of nuns, whose prayer and perpetual adoration would be for the grace of God on the mission work, was another step toward the realization of what was the essential for success. At one time he had thought of having perpetual adoration practiced by the priests of his Society. It was one of the minor points on which he and his co-founders had differed. He gave up the idea when he realized that this favorite idea of his would not fit in very well with the activities that would be demanded of his priests and Brothers. But the underlying principle he never gave up. Prayer was the lifeblood of apostolic endeavor, and Father Janssen's awareness of that fact and practical realization of it is one of the most significant traits in his character.

Chapter 27

O N NOVEMBER 5, 1907, Father Janssen celebrated his 70th birthday. Letters of congratulations, of
filial gratitude and affection came from all over the
world, for in the course of the past years the congregations which he had founded had grown with such
amazing rapidity that there were now some four hundred priests, seven hundred Brothers and five hundred
Sisters. And all of them seemed concerned that this
milestone in his career should not be passed without
an individual expression of devotion and joy from his
spiritual sons and daughters.

The mission seminary at Steyl fairly outdid itself to
commemorate the occasion. Bishop Henninghaus, who
headed the Society's Chinese Mission in South Shantung,
had been asked to grace the occasion with his presence.
It was his address which brought to a fitting close the
day of festivity. Before the assembled community and
a host of friends and benefactors he rose and an-

217

nounced: "I am here in the name of forty thousand Christians, who owe to you, Father Janssen, the grace of faith. I am here in the name of forty-three thousand catechumens, who are being taught the principles of Christian faith; and I am here to present to you the souls of more than one hundred and fifty thousand infants to whom the gates of heaven have been opened by baptism before death."

He went on to recount all the glorious things that the priests and Brothers of the Society of the Divine Word had done along with the Sister Servants of the Holy Ghost. These were the spiritual sons and daughters whose activity he had made possible; they were the ones who had caught the inspiration that held him, and with him had seen the vast vision of the fields white for the harvest, and had gone forth into its dangers, its loneliness and its death to work for the saving of souls.

Ultimately their successes were his. He had gathered them together, he had made possible by his own hard work and tireless prayers the training that equipped them to go forth and labor as apostles. He had put in their hands the cross that they were to announce, and he had put into their hearts the word that they were to speak, and he had grouped them under the standard of the Divine Word to show forth in their lives the things that they were to preach.

But he sat quietly now in the midst of all these encomiums and joy. A white-haired father in the midst of many children. He smiled benignly at their words of congratulation, their expressions of esteem and gratitude. The years of strenuous work and contradiction seemed at this moment like small payment for all that had been granted to him, and he understood now, in retrospect, how the wisdom of God had worked in his regard. In his heart he was saying: "It is indeed a blessing that the future is veiled from us. If it had been revealed to me, there would have been no merit in perseverance. He kept me in suspense. He gave me only enough strength to keep me from abandoning the idea, enough strength to complete the work once it was started." But the sense of gratefulness was so overwhelming at the realization of how graciously and abundantly the work of his hands had been blessed that when he rose to speak he could not find adequate utterance. All that he could say was that the goodness of God had blessed his endeavors, and that he was an imperfect and unworthy instrument.

But when the day was ended he wrote a letter of thanks to his far-distant ones in the mission fields for their words of thoughtfulness, and with them he shared more fully the thoughts that had crowded his heart on this festive day. "My cordial thanks for all the manifestations of love which you have sent me. I know that they come from souls who look upon me as their spiritual father, and whom I love in God, as my dear sons and helpers ... but I cannot accept all the praise that has been given me.... I am deeply aware of the duties I have toward all of you, and I want to beg your forgiveness for all the mistakes and faults I have committed in the discharge of my duties. I pray to God that, for the sake of the prayers which you have all sent up to his throne on this occasion, and despite singularities that may be mine, he will grant me the grace and power to fulfill these duties ever more and more faithfully.

"When I began the Society, the general opinion was that the work would fail. And those who thought so were perfectly right when they regarded my own insignificant person. Nevertheless, it has pleased the Lord to let the work succeed, and in a measure which I would never have thought possible."

Briefly he reviewed for them the work accomplished in the past thirty-two years, and exhorted all of them to continue to work in the same spirit. "The more you try to sanctify yourselves, the more will God bless your prayers and sacrifices. We serve a great and exalted King, who rewards his servants not royally but divinely."

Many of the letters that came to him for the event expressed the prayer and hope that his care and guidance might be granted to his group of fellow-workers for many more years to come. It is a conventional wish to express such a hope on one's birthday, but there was definite concern underlying the wish in Father Janssen's case. His health had been failing for some time, and there was an awareness of that fact in all who worked with him.

From his youth he had been sickly. At the time when he founded the first mission seminary at Steyl he was known to have a chest condition and was not expected to live very long. Several attacks of pneumonia left serious aftereffects. In 1894 he temporarily lost his speech. Despite that he had continued with his exhausting work, and, true to the determination he had expressed to them on his 70th birthday, he continued his heavy duties with even greater faithfulness.

During the following year he made a series of visits to all the different seminaries in Europe. His health deteriorated, and he returned to Steyl. He had always

220

made it a point to travel third-class, but at the solicitation of the fathers he finally capitulated. He rode second-class. It was a major triumph for the priest accompanying him when necessity made it imperative at one stage of the trip to use a cab, and Father Janssen submitted. After the ride Father Janssen gave the driver of the cab a goodly tip. His companion viewed the transaction with amazement, and Father Janssen, turning, caught the look upon his face. His eyes twinkled. "That often works better than the finest sermon," he explained.

The surprised priest agreed, but he was slightly confused at the love of poverty that travelled in the poorest railroad accommodations and yet tipped a cabman liberally. He had not as yet heard Father Janssen's principle for the attitude of the priest toward the working classes. "On a trip you ought to give a tip for everything above a mere answer to a question."

This inconsistency was very consistent. He was a poor man, who loved the poor.

The Society had grown impressively, but he remained unassuming, simple. Some of the younger members were not overly much enamored of this simplicity of his. To them Father Janssen now stood for something; they were more aware of his position and dignity seemingly than he was, and some of the rustic things he still adhered to irked their sense of proportion.

In particular there was the cumbersome piece of furniture that had been made for him during the pioneer days at Steyl — a bed with a wooden lid on it, so that it could serve in daytime for a table. This double-duty piece of furniture he had taken with him into the sacrosanct office of Superior General. It was not because of the crotchetiness of old age that refuses to walk any other ways except the ones it has always known, nor was it because of any utilitarian need. There were beds and tables enough for all now. But for him it was a reminder of the humble beginnings of the Society, it kept alive in his heart the memory of their poor beginnings, and it was an ever-present stimulus for that love of poverty which he wanted to be a characteristic of every one of his followers.

But their united admonitions as to the unsuitability and unseemliness of this ancient piece of bric-a-brac finally induced him to part with it — reluctantly.

In other respects, too, he yielded to the importunings of those about him. For the first time he allowed himself to be served special dishes and not merely the community fare. His health required a diet of special foods. He followed the doctor's orders, but what must have been very heart-warming for him was the evident solicitude of those about him. From the outset he had striven for that mutual charity among them all, that family spirit that was to him the essential for God's blessing and fruitful work. It is difficult to have a world-wide organization and not gradually have a formality, a casualness and indifference creep in. All are devoted to the same cause, but all are devoted to their particular sphere of activity, and gradually an unawareness of others as individuals can creep in. They become: the one in charge of the press; the Rector of the house; the Dean of Studies; the Novice-master, and so on down the line. Their interest in each other arises only when the discharge of their duties brings them together.

222

He wanted a family, not a collection of robotized functionaries. And when he came to a seminary on a visit his first question would be the question a father of a family would ask: "Is everyone well? Are there any sick?"

If anyone was ill, he would first visit them, would inquire if they were cared for adequately. He had a conviction that one of the functions of the sick, in God's Providence, was to draw more closely together the members of a household by the care and consideration for the ailing one.

When the influenza epidemic was ravaging Europe he preached a sermon one Sunday in the seminary that was hardest hit. "Many," he said, "are complaining that the Lord is punishing us. I say no; He is not punishing us, He is blessing us. The sick are a blessing for us all."

With his return to Steyl his own illness grew worse, but it seemed to make small change in his industrious days and his ever active prayer life. A slight stroke incapacitated his right side. He was no longer able to say Mass but continued his duties with the aid of his secretaries. To one of the superiors in the missions he dictated the following letter which gives a clear picture of how he was facing up to the trial that had befallen him. "You can imagine how gladly I would like to write you a few lines, but my hands are entirely paralyzed, and you will not take it ill that I must dictate to others what I have to say. I want to assure you that, despite what has now befallen me, I am content. For it is God alone who ordains everything. In case he should send me something even more trying I shall not lose courage. His Will be done in all things."

Gradually he regained his strength and was able to visit the chapel. He would spend many hours there. At midday, supported by a Brother, he would say the Stations of the Cross in the garden.

Mentally he was still alert, but often words to express his thoughts failed him. Then those around him had to guess what he meant, and he would try to assist them by means of signs.

His thumb and index fingers remained paralyzed so that he could not say Mass. On December 17 he sent the Brother Infirmarian to Father Bodems with the message that he wanted to see him at once.

Father Bodems found him standing, his face alight with a happy smile. Excitedly he whispered "I can; I can!"

"What do you mean?" asked Father Bodems.

Father Janssen raised his right hand and moved the thumb and index fingers. For a moment Father Bodems did not grasp the significance of this and then Father Janssen lifted both his hands, as the priest does at the elevation, and repeated: "I can; I can!"

Father Bodems then grasped that the Superior General was telling him that he would now be able to say Mass again. The following morning, assisted by one of the priests, he did say Mass, and continued to do so until the 4th of January.

On the 5th of January he was not able to rise from bed. His right side was completely paralyzed and the last rights were administered. He remained in a cheerful and contented mood.

A few days later the paralysis spread to the left side. The Prayers for the Dying were said, and Father

224

Janssen joined in the responses. He prayed aloud a great deal, at times seemingly unaware that others were present.

The hymn to the Holy Spirit, *Veni Sancti Spiritus,* kept murmuring from his lips, and always he seemed to place special stress upon the final phrase "grant eternal joy."

In the midst of his prayers, or in a lull, a small Latin phrase escaped him: *"et tui erant."* It seemed irrelevant, meaningless, yet it was as deeply prayerful and pleading as any of the formal prayers that came from his lips. Again and again it was spoken, and at last one of the priests placed it. *"Et tui erant"* — "because they are thine." It was a phrase from the prayer of Christ, the final prayer before He went forth to death. "I have manifested thy name to the men whom thou hast given me.... They were thine, and thou hast given them to me, and they have kept thy word ... I pray for them ... for those whom thou hast given me, *because they are thine."*

Christ's last prayer had been for the ones whom the Father had chosen to be His Apostles. In it He asked the Father to have a care of them, because they had done what the Father wanted, had accepted Him as the Father's Son, and believed in Him as the Messiah. He loved them, and so He prayed for them that they would grow in the knowledge and love of the Father and of Him. He had come for all, and He had prayed for all, but His last prayer before ascending the altar of the cross to redeem all, is an exclusive prayer for His Apostles, for the future propagators of the Gospel, for the one who will perpetuate the mystery of His redemption, for the heads of the Church.

225

He prays for them to become holy, to remain united, to become one with God, to abide in God's love. And the plea in His prayer is founded on these simple words, so eloquent and so irresistible to the heart of the Father: "because they are thine."

This was the prayer that hovered in Arnold Janssen's consciousness as the moment of passage from life to death drew near. All his life through he had prayed that the Heart of Jesus might live in the hearts of men, and if a man's last moments are revelatory of his deepest soul and of what it is that makes him what he is, then these simple words, repeated by Arnold Janssen, indicate that the Heart of Christ lived truly in his own heart. The fears of death and whatever might lie beyond seemed not to touch his last moments, and, even for a man who had lived spiritually, those final moments could well have been a time of dread, for the burden of his office had placed in his hands the disposition of large sums of money as well as the responsibility for many men's lives and careers. But he thought nothing of this, only of others, the ones whom the loving Father had given him to share in the work. They were dear to him, with the affection that is above earth and natural affection. He had led them into the desires of Christ's heart, as best he could, with his halting words and imperfect efforts. The vision of Christ's vast thoughts and yearnings had always been so far above his ability to express or drive home. But he had tried. And now that he was leaving them, they would be as sheep without a shepherd. He knew them and their weaknesses, but he knew, too, their deep, driving desire to follow the Will of God, even as he had. What could he say that would draw down the guidance, the help, the loving aid that they would need? What prayer could he say that would be potent to turn the Father's eyes upon his children. The words of Christ, the words that Christ had used when He too went away and left His Apostles to face the preaching of the word without the physical presence of the Word ... *et tui erunt....*

His life had opened in the mysterious warmth of the words of faith that opened St. John's Gospel, and now it closes in the trustful pleading, the abiding faith of the same sacred writer. He would go from the world in the faith that he had entered; he would depart, believing in the Word, who was in the beginning with God, the Word who was God, and who would care for his spiritual sons and daughters "because they were His."

The last word he spoke was the name of Jesus. On the 15th of January, 1909, he passed away, quietly and without any struggle.

He was buried at Steyl, in the quiet fields beside the quiet river. Here, thirty-three years ago he had begun his work, on a practically abandoned little spot, and his sole capital had been his confidence in God. The seed he had planted had grown and spread even unto all the faraway places of the world. But the buildings that sprung up, the public acclaim that came to him, and the wide-spread organization he ruled over made no change in him. The poor knew him as one who cared for them, the people of the countryside looked on him with awe as the man who had built huge buildings with no money, priests and bishops had known him as a pious, persevering man, but they knew little of him save what they had seen. It was one of his own sons who opened up wide the goodness of this unsung dead: "He always let us share his joys, but his crosses he bore alone."

227

Chapter 28

THE TWO individuals held up to us by the Church as the ideals, the patrons for missionary endeavor are an amazing study in contrasts. St. Francis Xavier was a man of abounding energy, ceaseless activity, endless journeyings, who baptized thousands of pagans and worked many miracles. St. Therese of Lisieux was a Carmelite, a slip of a girl who never saw a pagan, whose whole world was the four walls of the cloister at Lisieux, who wrote a little book, and died very young.

Totally different, yet completely the same were these two. The Church has made no mistake in putting the hidden away Carmelite by the side of the world-famous, much-travelled missionary, for the both of them possess, in an eminent degree, the quality that makes for outstanding and truly successful apostolic endeavor. Both of them were deeply interior souls, completely absorbed in the desires and aims of the Divine Mission-

228

ary. She in her prayer life, in her little way of duties love-filled. He in his prayer life, and large activities love-filled. Both walked the ways of greatness, for their ways were God's way.

And by that standard Arnold Janssen was a great missionary. There was in him the happy conjunction of a driving intensity of action and a profound depth of quiet. The eyes mirror that curious disparity, the alert, wide-open glance of one, the soft, inward reflectiveness of the other. And beneath those two qualities lay a deeply interior life, a life bound up intimately with the desires of the Sacred Heart. That the Kingdom of Christ might come in the hearts of all men ... that was the consuming hope and ideal that burned brightly in his heart. He labored for that goal, in the way manifested to him, in season and out of season. Buildings, possessions, fields of activity, new enterprises, additional congregations seemed to multiply about him, but the multiplicity of these external things, the success attending the ventures he put his hand to were only signs, outward signs of the inward spirit from which they sprang.

Good as are all the things he achieved, what is of greater importance for our fast-moving age is the spirit of the man himself. For he was very much a child of our day, interested deeply in the swift-striding advances of science and all the new techniques and possibilities they offered. He used them unhesitatingly, eagerly, making of science an ally of religion. But other men have done the same thing, perhaps better, and with greater acclaim. In that he is not unique. But he is unique in his own person. Though activities multiplied about him, quiet only deepened within him. He stood

229

in the midst of the whirlpool of eddying life, was part of it, but not absorbed by it. He retained his peace of soul, his personal integrity.

Up and down the length of the land he journeyed, through Germany, Holland, Austria-Hungary, Switzerland, back and forth to Rome. His external activity was unceasing, his internal devotion uninterrupted. The spirit of prayer seemed to deepen within him as his other activities multiplied. In his person the restless drive of the ardent apostle seemed to blend with the deep withdrawal of the contemplative. Engrossed with the plans for building mission seminaries, absorbed with the task of founding a religious order of priests and Brothers, in framing the constitutions of a twofold congregation of Sisters, purchasing property, directing the press, counselling and supporting his missionaries in far-off countries, he yet remains unpretentious and hidden, making his whole life one of ordered desire that the desires of Christ's heart may be fulfilled.

There were safeguards, in the midst of his activity, to keep firm and clear before his mind the one thing necessary. The Quarter-Hour Prayer lifting his mind and heart above the work to the One for whom it was done. Regularly, mechanically at first it had been, but the mechanicalness of it soon disappeared and the lifting of his thoughts and desires to the indwelling God became as easy and regular as breathing. His hands were busy, but so, too, was his heart.

Before dictating important letters he would kneel down and pray. If he promised in a letter to pray for someone, he would say to his secretary: "Now let us kneel down and say the promised prayer at once."

Activity did not so absorb him that piety died. The

230

thousand realities of each day's material projects were never allowed to obscure the great Reality.

And that is his peculiar charm for us in this hurrying age. It is possible to be engaged in the tasks of everyday life, the earning of a livelihood in shop and office and factory, and yet bring to the drudgery of our tasks the romance of a great faith. Growth in possessions and progress in technical skills, advancement to places of importance, are not, and never can be, as important as growth in personal greatness, progress in prayer, advancement in the awareness, dependence and friendship of God. You grow personally, if you grow Godwards; and you can grow Godwards by work that is prayer.

There is light and shadow in Arnold Janssen's life, bright lights and deep shadows, there is joy and sorrow, there is work and hardship, patience and toil, prayer, tireless prayer, and love, a great love. All these things are there and many more, because he was simple, and like all simple things, profoundly complex. He was so humble yet so stubborn, so unpretentious yet so daring, so provincial in his ways of speech and travel, a typical peasant, yet so much a citizen of the world with his eyes and thoughts in the remotest corners of the globe, so saving and economical in dress and food and habits of living, yet handling vast sums of money with the indifferent calm of a great financier, so dry as dust a scientist and mathematician, yet permeated with mysticism. He was a lover of the natural sciences, and yet a lover of prayer and mortification. A child of his country, a child of all countries. A son of the soil, who took delight in machinery. He was impractical, yet very practical, forging swords for the modern warfare of the spirit — the press, the retreats, the modern approach to mission work.

231

And the solution to the seemingly endless contradictions in him was, of course, his simplicity. He was a simple man, he had one view, one aim and only one — and that was the Will of God. The qualities of his mind and heart were all bent toward that end. While awaiting the manifestation of that Will he would delay, and that made others think that he was unable to grasp a need, unable to make a decision. So in their opinion he had no administrative ability. But when the issue was clear, then he moved quietly, firmly, perseveringly, so perseveringly that to others it was stubbornness, for they did not realize that what God willed was the be-all and end-all of his life. No sacrifice of time or labor, of pain or opposition was too great when it was a question of this.

So, too, with all the other seeming contradictions in the man. The key once held, the locks open easily. We know now why this great lover of the missions never set foot in a mission land; why the one who was so enamored of activity could sit back and wait; why the one who was a peasant and slow of speech could seek out and confer with aristocrats and Cardinals, with Popes and even an Emperor.

But the understanding of that aspect of him does not readily make clear why it was that such as he was chosen for the task that he fulfilled. A herald is one who announces or represents a person. We would imagine that the Divine Word would have chosen for the task of proclaiming His Person and His word, and for grouping men together who were to be messengers of the Word, a man who was master of the art of both the written and spoken word, a man who mirrored in his own person much of the grace of the Divine Word.

232

Instead He chose a man who, in the words of another priest, "can't even speak."

God's works are frequently manifested by the seeming inability of the insruments used.

The external qualities that the world so readily pays homage to were not evident in Arnold Janssen. But dedicated so intimately as he was to the aspirations and desires of Christ it would be impossible for the grace and greatness of the Divinity not to overflow upon him. Greatness there was, greatness as befitted a chosen one, greatness as befitted a selected herald of the Word. But the greatness was within. And if at times it gleamed forth it was never by design; for the greatness of this man was an artless simplicity, a simple yes, yes, or a no, no — an eager affirmation to whatever was the design of God, a stubborn implacable denial for all that was not.

He would have all his sons and daughters as simple as that, and all whom they would care for and bring to the light of faith. For that was the heart of Christ: "The things that please my Father I do always," and in that was the realization of his motto "That the heart of Christ might live in the hearts of men."

The vast field of foreign mission endeavor was the work of God Himself. He came down to earth to perform it, and he entrusted it primarily to His Apostles, but not to them alone. The work of the missions was for every Christian. It was a work for all. Arnold Janssen knew that, and he tried to stir up all Catholics to share in it. He rejoiced when other congregations entered into the work, for it was a work above individual desires. The work of the apostle always had to be, if it were to carry out the designs of God. Apostolic work had to be devoid of self, for then only could the full greatness and glory of the gospel shine through. It was not merely that the unbeliever could then see in the missionary's own person the living example of the truth he preached, but the grace of the Holy Spirit could come down in abundance upon the missionary's efforts. For when self went out, God could come in.

In all things he was ordinary. It was as though God wanted a man that our modern world could understand, efficient, far-seeing, firm in his decisions, hard-headed like any business man in pursuit of his aims. But all these qualities, so appealing to the modern mind, were directed, primarily and steadfastly toward eternal values.

And that is why there is a wider implication to Arnold Janssen's life than just the arousing of interest in foreign missionary endeavor. There is in it a call to every man, and a reminder, that the things of time and their pursuit are only of value insofar as they are tied to timeless values. For it is that which gives purpose to everything we do, deepening all the talents, the thought and labors we bring to our endeavors. It is that which makes it worthy "to spend and be spent" in them. For in the loss of self, in the exhaustion of our energies there is complete fulfillment, in the loss of life there is eternal gain.